David Livingstone

WHO WAS . . . ?

DAVID LIVINGSTONE

THE LEGENDARY EXPLORER

BY **AMANDA MITCHISON**

ILLUSTRATED BY **JAMES NUNN**

 **SHORT BOOKS**

First published in 2003 by
Short Books
15 Highbury Terrace
London N5 1UP

10 9 8 7 6 5 4 3 2 1

Illustrations on pages 31 & 100:
The David Livingstone
Centre Blantyre, Glasgow.

A CIP catalogue record for this book
is available from the British Library.

ISBN 1-904095-30-5

Printed in Great Britain by
Bookmarque Ltd, Croydon, Surrey

For James Dawson
Best of Boys

'Dr Livingstone, I presume?...'

The journalist Henry Morton Stanley was a fierce little man who liked to do things in style. So when his editor told him to go into the heart of Africa to find the long lost explorer David Livingstone, and to spare no expense in doing so, Stanley took his boss at his word. He set out with 193 porters and six tons of luggage including 20 miles of cloth, a million beads, two collapsible boats and a number of giant kettles to warm the water for his baths.

It was a long, arduous journey: seven months on foot and donkey (his horses perished within days of setting out) all the way from the east African coast, through war zones and great rains, to the hills overlooking Lake Tanganyika. But Stanley never let his standards of personal valeting slip.

And on the morning of 10th November 1871, he was particularly fastidious about his appearance. He knew this was his big day. A few hours walk from now he would be entering the lakeside town of Ujiji where, he had heard on his travels, an old, sick white man was staying. If that man was Dr Livingstone – the famous Livingstone who had crossed the African continent twice and who had been gone so long that newspapers had even published obituaries* – then Stanley would have the scoop of a lifetime. And he, too, would be famous.

Stanley ordered his Arab boy Selim to oil his boots and see that his pith helmet was freshly chalked, with a new pagaree* folded around the rim. He put on his neatly pressed white flannel suit – the waist band was a little loose now, thanks to that terrible attack of dysentery back on the Makata swamp. He checked the suit very carefully, stroking the fabric with his small, neatly manicured hands. If there were so much as a fleck of dirt on his trousers, he would have personally dog-whipped Selim.

A few hours later, when the expedition was just outside Ujiji, Stanley stopped. He gave his white suit a final inspection and unfurled an American flag, giving it to a large, handsome porter to carry at the front of the caravan* as a standard bearer. Then, with his men firing volleys of shots to herald his arrival, Stanley strode into the little town.

Stanley looked as crisp and dapper as a Victorian gentleman stepping out for a game of lawn tennis, but he felt very nervous. Was Livingstone really in the town? And, if so, did he *want* to be found? No white man – black men didn't count in Stanley's eyes – had seen Dr Livingstone in six years, and there had been countless rumours that he was dead.

The sound of the guns brought the townspeople out on to the street and, in a great hubbub of dust and noise, everyone jostled excitedly around the newcomers. But when Stanley reached the main square the crowd suddenly parted. There, hobbling shakily towards him, was the famous explorer. Stanley had seen photographs of Livingstone and knew immediately that this was his man. He recognised the walrus moustache, the down-turned mouth, the mournful eyes, and of course the little blue peaked cap he always wore.

But, oh how different Livingstone looked now!

Stanley had expected a stern, vigorous man with a firm handshake and upright bearing. But this Livingstone was a pathetic-looking figure: a hunched, trembling old man with a pale, lined face and a walking-stick. Livingstone's tunic was frayed and bleached, his eyes had that starved, sunken look of the very ill and he had lost nearly all his teeth. He was only 58.

The crowd fell silent in expectation. Stanley marched forward, raised his hat and said, with a slight tremor in his voice, 'Dr Livingstone, I presume?'

CHAPTER ONE

It wasn't yet dawn when 13-year-old David Livingstone awoke. The factory hooter at Blantyre Mills would go in half an hour. So there was just time for prayers, a nice cold boiled potato and possibly a relieving sit on the foul earth closet* at the back of the tenement.

David and his older brother John folded their blankets, pushed their truckle beds under their parents' bed and splashed their faces with cold water. By the standards of Scotland in the 1830s, the Livingstones were sticklers for hygiene. They regularly wetted the parts of themselves that showed and, unlike most of their neighbours, they did not share their small kitchen-cum-living-room-cum-bedroom with any poultry or pigs.

With the truckle beds out of the way, there was just enough space in the room for father, mother, John,

David and the three smaller children to stand around the little table and thank the Lord for his bountifulness. Father led the prayers and recited a psalm. Afterwards mother handed round the cold potatoes and gave each of the boys a teaspoonful of laxative Senna syrup. Mr Livingstone believed in the Word of God and never let drink, or tobacco or novels over the threshold. But Mrs Livingstone really put her faith in regular bowel movements and she was to pass this abiding interest on to her second son.

David collected his breakfast and his lunch – oatcakes, cold kale and a tiny piece of cheese – folded them in an old handkerchief, and set off for work in the spinning factory. These days he was most careful not to use paper – John had recently been caned for disrespect after he wrapped his square of porridge in a tract* entitled 'Practical Christianity'.

Outside it was still dark and the rain was falling. There was a throng of men, women and children also making their way to the factory and most had their heads muffled up in scarves or shawls to try and keep dry. But Livingstone didn't seem to notice the rain. Instead all his attention was drawn to the night sky. A few months ago he had borrowed a small book about astronomy from the factory library and was now able to identify most of the major constellations and stars. Up above him that morning he could see the plough and nearby the pole star was shining bright. A little way off he could make out the squiggly 'M' shape of Cassiopeia, and there was Lyra shining far down near the horizon. Livingstone continued walking, his face turned up to the sky and his feet splashing straight through the puddles.

At 6 o'clock in the morning the hooter duly sounded and Livingstone and his workmates made their way to a huge room filled with enormous pieces of machinery called 'spinning-jennies'. In the centre of each jenny was a mass of cotton fluff from which scores of little threads came whirring off on to spindles. Livingstone was a 'piecer' – his job was to repair any breaks in the thread. With practice he had learnt to tell when a thread was beginning to fray or get too thin – and the knack was always to repair or 'piece' together the thread before it broke completely.

Within minutes the jennies were in full swing, with shuttles and wheels clattering and whirring and great clouds of steam hissing up through vents in the floor.

Livingstone propped a small green book entitled *Ruddiman's Rudiments of Latin* on the side of the jenny farthest from where his master spinner, Mr Seagrove, sat.

Livingstone opened his book on page 32. '*Hic haec hoc, hi hae haec*', he read. Then he repeated the words as his eyes scanned across the reels and bobbins. A thread over the far side of the second jenny was getting dangerously thin. Livingstone clambered under the lower part of the machine. '*Hic haec hoc*,' he muttered to himself as he took off the bobbin, licked the thread, twiddled the two ends together. '*Hic haec hoc*', he rewound the spool and reinserted it in its slot. Then he crawled back under the machine. '*Hic haec hoc, hi hae haec.*' He fixed another thread on the way and returned to his *Rudiments of Latin*.

The morning wore on. He had memorised two irregular declensions before the factory stopped for breakfast. And by lunchtime he had revised his verbs and moved on to his parallel translations – he had done the dictionary work the night before between 10pm and midnight. And that had been before he had perused his geological samples, which were always referred to by his mother as 'Davey's dirty staines*'.

Livingstone continued his work. He would read a sentence and then scan the threads again. Read. Scan. Read. Scan. So it went on hour after hour after hour, as the afternoon light faded and the bobbins grew fat with thread and the pages of *Ruddiman's Rudiments* of Latin swelled in the hot, wet heat.

Nothing would put the boy off. Once, when there was a loud splash followed by a sharp squeal, Livingstone didn't even look up from *Caesar's Gallic Wars*. For he knew that was the sound of Mr Seagrove sousing little peaky-faced Euphemia Carruthers with the cold water from a fire bucket. She always did fall asleep in the early evening. Lucky for her that Mr Seagrove only thrashed boys! And even when the MacLeod twins – who were no better than they ought to be – threw bobbins at his grammar book and dislodged it from the jenny, Livingstone ignored their jeers and simply picked it up, scanned his threads again, and returned to his page.

Finally, blessed release came. At eight o'clock in the evening the last hooter sounded. Livingstone's calves were aching – he had crawled and clambered nearly 20 miles under and over the jennies – but he was exultant.

By the end of the week he would have finished Chapter Six. One day he would be able to read the classics! One day he would be educated and fit for better things!

There was a skip to his stride as he made his way to the factory schoolroom. For now – praise be to God! – it was time for his two-hour Latin lesson.

CHAPTER TWO

The young David Livingstone agonised about his soul: Had the Holy Spirit touched him? What was God's purpose for him? Surely he had been singled out for something? If so, what?

And then, in his late teens, he found a vocation. He would become a missionary, a minister sent out to foreign lands to spread Christianity. Only Livingstone went one step further — he wished to become a *medical* missionary, sent abroad to cure bodies as well as souls. This solved a problem for Livingstone. Becoming a medical missionary would allow him to follow the Lord's will while still continuing with the scientific pursuits he enjoyed so much.

But it wasn't easy for a boy from the mills to gain an education. And Livingstone was 23 years old before he had earned enough in the factory to pay for his studies, and enrol as a medical student in Glasgow. Even then, life continued to be a struggle. Livingstone spent his holidays working in the factory. Every weekend he went home to his parents, and on Monday mornings he rose at five in the morning in order to walk the eight miles to Glasgow in time for his first lecture of the day.

Finally, in 1838, after two years at Glasgow, Livingstone was accepted by the London Missionary Society who sent him for two years more training in medicine and theology in England. His theology tutors found him uncouth and awkward: a sombre, stodgy young man obsessed with his bowels. He was self-conscious about speaking in public, partly because of his thick Scottish accent and partly because of a slight speech impediment – Livingstone had an overly large uvula* which made his voice gruff and indistinct. Consequently he was a poor preacher, and the first time he was due to give a sermon he suffered a fit of nerves and bolted from the church.

Yet Livingstone was determined to become a missionary; he pictured himself venturing into unknown lands and saving souls. He had originally dreamed of going to

China, but this hope was shattered with the outbreak of the Opium War. Eventually the London Missionary Society suggested a placement in southern Africa and he was very keen to go. Africa too was an unknown land – at that time maps of the continent left the interior mostly blank – and, in London, Livingstone had been to an anti-slavery lecture which had fired him up with a sense of purpose.

So in December 1840 Livingstone, aged 27, set sail from London. The Britain he left behind was going through a period of rapid change: the electric telegraph had just been developed, the first postage stamps (the 'penny blacks') were being issued and steam trains were beginning to replace the old stage coaches. At this date, Britain also had an empire – the young Queen Victoria ruled over parts of India and Canada and all of Australia. This didn't mean, however, that the problems back home had been solved: here the poor lived in misery and degradation. In 1840, people in the town of Paisley, just a few miles from Livingstone's home, were dying of starvation.

Livingstone would not return to Britain for 16 years. During his absence, the technological advances would forge ahead. The explorer would return to find telegraph lines laid throughout the country and the houses of the rich lit by gaslight. The conditions of the poor, however, would improve only very slightly. The spinners and piecers back in Hamilton would still be eking out a most meagre living, one family to a room.

***

Nothing in his bleak and cramped childhood had prepared Livingstone for Africa. None of his books had brought home to him the dust and burnt earth, the crawling heat of the afternoons, and the lemony smell of the khaki weed. But Livingstone was surprised, above all, by the sheer size and slowness of the vast continent.

Soon after his arrival in Cape Town, he began his long trek north to Kuruman, the settlement built by the renowned missionary Robert Moffat in Bechuanaland – in what is today South Africa.

For weeks and weeks his ox-drawn wagon trundled through rolling savannah* and then on into endless sandy flatlands with nothing but occasional rocks, dried-out river-beds and spiny bushes.

LIVINGSTONE'S EARLY
JOURNEYS
1841-1852

Livingstone was surprised, too, by the natives – how they stared so boldly at him. He tried very hard not to stare back. He had been warned of their nakedness: they wore nothing except cloaks and little leather aprons which only just covered their private parts. But he had never expected the Africans to be *shiny* – the tribesmen and women, he soon discovered, smeared themselves in oil and then rolled their limbs in a metallic powder. The process reminded him of how his mother back in Blantyre would stop scones sticking in the oven by greasing the baking trays with lard, and then dusting them with flour.

And Livingstone was even more surprised by the white missionaries he met in the outposts – what gossips they were! What backbiters! How little they seemed to accomplish! Having read the missionary literature, Livingstone had expected Kuruman to be a large, bustling settlement with hundreds of happy black Christians and many nearby settlements ripe for conversion. For Robert Moffat, when they had met in London, had spoken of 'the smoke rising from the fires of a thousand villages to the north'.

But when Livingstone finally arrived at Kuruman, he

found only a *tiny* village with a little church, a few bungalows, some fruit trees and irrigated fields. There were 350 native inhabitants, but only a tenth of them were baptised. And all around the village lay more of the same flat, arid plains without a soul in sight.

Moffat had devoted 20 years to building up Kuruman. Was that all he had achieved? Just 35 more souls in the everlasting arms of Jesus? And where, in any case, were these smoking villages to the north?

***

So Livingstone went north. Over the next two years he made a series of journeys up into the uncharted lands of the Bakhatla and the Bakwain tribes. The first trip he did with a fellow missionary called Edwards, but after that he preferred to go just with his African bearers and his wagon and oxen.

On his travels Livingstone was welcomed by the local chiefs. They knew that the strange white rainmaker-medicine man with the thin slithery hair and the bird beak of a nose had *power*. He had beads, he had cloth, he had *guns*. He also had other magic: he had a small flat round stone that he kept tucked in his chest clothes. This stone whirred like a cricket and had on its front little marks and two little sticks that went round and round. And then there was the even more wonderful magic thing – a bigger, thinner flat round stone that shone like a still pond. Anyone who looked in it saw their own face looking back out at them.

Livingstone, for his part, quickly developed a knack for relating to the African people. He didn't mind the children stroking his strangely thin hair and he smiled when a woman, who couldn't quite believe his protuberant nose was real, touched him on the face and ran away squealing with laughter. He also let the Africans look at his watch and make faces at themselves in his little hand mirror. How they laughed when he brought out his cutlery at mealtimes or knelt on the ground to say his prayers.

Livingstone was grieved to discover how little interest the local Africans had in Christianity, but as he mended their decrepit rifles and showed them how to build irrigation systems to water their crops, he would slip in a few words about the teaching of Jesus. The Africans would smile back and nod and present the doctor with yet another small, glue-eyed baby in need of treatment.

Livingstone suspected that he was being taken advantage of, and gradually changed his approach. He became haughtier – the natives must realise it was a *privilege* to have him help them. When he arrived in a village, he would draw a circle in the earth and sit in the middle and demand that no one come into the circle without his permission.

It was also most important, Livingstone realised, to show no fear. And showing no fear meant *feeling* no fear. After all, if God had sent him on this special mission to convert the heathen, then God would also protect him. He must banish the very thought that anything could go wrong.

So on the fateful day when he came to the huge black basalt rocks where the Bakaa tribe lived, Livingstone didn't change his pace. The Bakaa had an evil reputation among neighbouring tribes, and a few years before they had poisoned a white trader called Gibson and three of his men. One of the men had survived the poisoning but the Bakaa had strangled him with a leather thong. Then they had burnt down the trader's wagons for the iron in the nails and had eaten his oxen.

But Livingstone cast this story to the back of his mind, and walked slowly on up the narrow ravine towards the village perched on a ledge in the cliff face. From time to time he looked up, expecting to see a crowd of natives gazing down on him and his bearers. But there was no one.

When Livingstone walked into the centre of the village, he realised that the inhabitants had fled. Only the chief and two of his attendants were there to greet him.

Livingstone squatted down on the earth opposite the chief, who smiled at him uneasily. During the usual long wait while food was prepared, Livingstone concentrated on remaining relaxed. He tried hard not to look too often at the chief, whose eyes were flitting from side to side like an antelope grazing in high grass. All three of the tribesmen were wearing necklaces made of gun parts and bits from old tin jugs, which once no doubt belonged to the unfortunate Gibson.

At last some porridge arrived. Without a moment's hesitation, Livingstone picked up his bowl and slurped heartily. As he did so, the chief and his attendants suddenly started to relax and, in the distance, villagers emerged from the shadows among the rocks.

After he had finished his gruel, Livingstone yawned and stretched his arms and then, begging leave from the chief, he lay down and went to sleep. Soon there was a crowd of excited villagers around his prostrate body.

Livingstone spent several days with the Bakaa. He never liked the look of the people much – those Gibson booty necklaces were everywhere – but they treated him kindly and he came to no harm.

***

Apart from hostile tribes, there was another great danger in Africa: wild animals. Two years after his arrival, Livingstone and Roger Edwards, an older missionary, started up a new settlement 220 miles northeast of Kuruman at a site called Mabotsa. Unlike Kuruman, Mabotsa was in hospitable terrain with woodlands and a plentiful supply of water. But Mabotsa was also plagued with lions.

One day Livingstone was out digging a water ditch when some Bakhatla tribesmen ran screaming to him. He must come, they cried, and help them kill a lion that was attacking their sheep. Livingstone grabbed his gun and followed the men across the valley.

The lion was crouched on top of a small rock. Livingstone approached, fired both barrels into the animal but failed to kill it. He shouted to the men to wait, and was just ramming the new bullets into his gun when he heard a cry and turned to see the lion springing through the air towards him.

The lion came down on Livingstone's shoulder, ripping asunder his tartan tweed jacket, mauling the flesh underneath and bringing him tumbling to the ground. Then, sinking its fangs into his arm, the lion shook him violently – just as a dog does when he catches a rat.

This shaking left Livingstone strangely numb and dreamy. The bone in his arm was now in splinters and his shoulder was a gory mass, yet he felt no pain, and no fear. Of course he was aware of what was happening – he could hear the lion growling horribly close to his ear and could smell the animal's rank breath. He knew, too, that his body was in agony and that he was very close to death.

But it was as if all feeling and distress had been simply shaken out of him. He wondered if this was God mercifully making his death easier. And when this lion did get round to eating him, where would he begin? The arm? The leg? The buttock?

But at that moment the lion became distracted.

Livingstone could feel the lion's paw on the back of his head and the weight was crushing him into the ground, so he turned his face a fraction. Now he could see that the lion was looking up. The animal's great yellow barley-sugar eyes were fixed on Livingstone's servant Mebalwe, who was shouting and pointing a pistol.

Mebalwe fired two shots, but each time there was only a dull click as the pistol misfired. The lion abandoned Livingstone and dived at Mebalwe, biting him in the thigh. Then one of the Bakwain hunters came forward and speared the lion. In a rage, the creature turned round and attacked his new assailant, goring him in the shoulder.

A second later the lion collapsed dead on the ground. Livingstone's bullets had finally taken effect.

***

For weeks Livingstone lay in agony in his hut, too ill and weak to move. Edwards had cleaned Livingstone's wounds and picked out the bits of tartan tweed with a pair of pliers. Under Livingstone's instructions, the missionary had also made a splint and tried to set the bone. But Livingstone's break was messy, and the wounds suppurated* in the heat.

Very gradually he began to recover, though the arm would always look odd and he would never be able to raise it above his shoulder. Livingstone noticed with interest that his wounds were healing far faster than Mebalwe's or those of the other tribesman who had also been mauled in the shoulder. He put this down to the curative effects of his tartan jacket, which had helped clean infection off the lion's teeth and claws before it broke through into his flesh. Nothing, he believed, could beat a good tweed in the tropics.

After three months, Livingstone returned to Kuruman to finish his convalescence at Robert Moffat's house. Day after day Livingstone sat on a rocking-chair on the veranda and watched the eldest Moffat daughter Mary bustle around bringing him tea and barking orders in Setswana* to the African washerwomen.

Mary was no beauty. She was a stout, dumpy woman with a long nose and a parboiled complexion. She had a

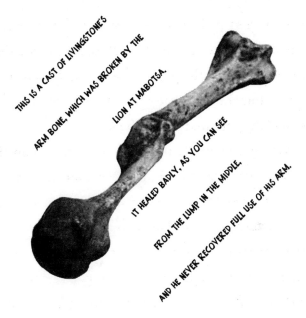

THIS IS A CAST OF LIVINGSTONE'S ARM BONE, WHICH WAS BROKEN BY THE LION AT MABOTSA. IT HEALED BADLY, AS YOU CAN SEE FROM THE LUMP IN THE MIDDLE, AND HE NEVER RECOVERED FULL USE OF HIS ARM.

thick, fleshy back and her hands were rough as sand-paper. But she was amiable and useful. She was a dab hand at making candles, she could run a primary school and sew clothes. And she was well accustomed to the hardship of outback Africa.

Livingstone told himself that was what he needed: a sturdy, commonsense wife, not one of those pretty, flighty ladies from England who would pine for their carriages and their balls. Oh, it had been such a lonely life out there, digging ditches in Mabotsa! And Mary Moffat did make a lovely carbolic soap.

One day, towards the end of his stay, he saw Mary Moffat sitting with the family mending basket under an almond tree in the orchard. Livingstone strode out purposefully. There was no point pretending to stumble upon her by chance – he must make his purpose clear from the very start and be done with the awkward business as fast as possible.

As he came into the orchard, Livingstone gave a sharp little cough and Mary Moffat looked up, gave him a quick smile, and bowed her head once more over her darning.

Livingstone's tongue seemed to have expanded to fill his whole mouth, just as it had when he had been parched with thirst on his travels. How did one broach the topic? It was worse than giving his first sermon, but this time he must not bolt.

Livingstone gave another cough and began, 'Miss Moffat, during these days of my convalescence, I have noted with approval your sober and amiable disposition. I must remark on how very tolerably you fulfil those womanly tasks assigned to you. These are most estimable qualities.'

Mary Moffat, flushing with pleasure at the faint praise, kept her head bowed over her mending.

'Now these days of leisure, Miss Moffat, have also given me the opportunity for much reflection. And various considerations' – here Livingstone eyed the almond trunk very firmly – 'have led me to the conclusion that the time has come to enter into matrimonial union.'

At this point Mary Moffat looked up, but Livingstone raised his hand to indicate that he had not finished.

'Allow me to explain.' he continued. 'I currently receive a salary of £75 a year from the London Missionary Society. The society, as you are perhaps aware, provide an increased rate of £100 per annum for their incumbents who marry. I believe this would be more than adequate to run a prudent household upon, would it not?

'Oh most certainly Mr Livingstone,' replied Mary Moffat.

'Then we are in agreement?'

Mary Moffat now looked very pink.

'Miss Moffat – Mary – you will do me the honour of becoming my wife?'

'Yes, with pleasure, Mr Livingstone.' Miss Moffat rose from her bench.

'Good! Then the matter is settled,' said Livingstone, giving his arm to his new fiancée. The satisfied couple then went for a brief walk around the orchard, where they spent a happy half-hour discussing oxen and supplies and suitable dates, and other such important matters.

The word 'love' never crossed their lips.

CHAPTER THREE

After their wedding, David and Mary Livingstone returned to Mabotsa. However Livingstone had quarrelled with Edwards, and soon the couple moved again 40 miles north to Chonuane, where Sechele, a chief of the Bakwena tribe and a noted local rainmaker, was living.

But here too there were problems. The drought was drying up the local springs, and within a year Sechele was forced to move his people north west to Kolobeng, a bleak site perched on a ridge of red ironstone by a small river. The Livingstones, who now had Robert, a toddler, and Agnes, a three-month-old baby, followed in their wagon.

Kolobeng was to be the nearest the Livingstones ever came to a settled home. At first the couple and their two tiny children lived in a rickety, fly-filled hut. But after a year Livingstone finally finished making the walls and roof of a stone house – doors and windows would have to wait – and the family moved in.

They became quite house-proud. Livingstone decorated the interior with antlers and, as a great extravagance, ordered a sofa from Cape Town. Mrs Livingstone smeared the walls with cow-dung every week, to kill the fleas and settle the dust.

Mary Livingstone milked the cows, ground the meal* and baked her own bread in an old hollowed-out ant-hill. When the family ran short of zebra meat, they ate caterpillars, frogs and locusts, which, Livingstone complained, were very constipating.

Meanwhile Livingstone looked after the crops and the wagons and the guns and the cattle. Then in the evening, after his day of hard manual labour, he would give Sechele reading lessons. The chief was a good pupil. He learnt the alphabet – lower- and upper-case – in just two days and compiled his own spelling book. He raced through *The Pilgrim's Progress* several times over and loved reading aloud, especially from the Book of Isaiah. He gave up hunting to devote more time to his books and grew quite chubby in the process.

Chief Sechele was eager for knowledge about the West. He also adored European clothes and wore them in interesting combinations. His wardrobe included a mackintosh, a pair of boots, a duffel jacket, an ancient red coat, an assortment of hats and a suit of clothes, made out of hartebeest skin by Livingstone's mother-in-law, Mrs Moffat. The hartebeest coat was a little tight and the hartebeest trousers a bit short, but it was still a very splendid outfit.

Behind the gifts and the reading lessons, there was, of course, a motive: Livingstone was trying to spread the gospel. If he could only convert Sechele then the whole tribe could be his!

So, every evening, Livingstone worked on Sechele. It was a very gradual process, but eventually, after many gifts and much persuasion, Livingstone made his first small victory: he convinced the chief to give up his rain-making ceremonies.

The local people were appalled. And when the drought returned and the trees died and the corn failed and the River Kolobeng dried to a dribble, they blamed Livingstone. For was it not the white man who had encouraged their chief to turn away from his traditional beliefs and stop rainmaking?

The old men of the village pleaded with Livingstone to let Sechele make rain again. 'Why does the white man use medicines if he does not believe in their power? He does not know our medicines, just as we don't know his. God has given many things to the white man which he has not given to the black man, but has he not also given things to the black man that he has not given to the white man – such as the knowledge of trees that can make rain? We don't ask you to give up your wagons. Why should we give up rainmaking?'

When Livingstone replied that only God could make rain, the exasperated villagers would retort 'Of course we know that. It is God who cures diseases too. Whoever heard of one who could cure when death came? We pray to God using the medicines which he has given us. And so it is with the rain. *We* don't make the rain. God does.'

And then came the day when Sechele made the momentous decision that he would take up Christianity and renounce four of his five wives. For Sechele this was not only a personal sacrifice, but politically dangerous. A man's importance and his standing in the tribe depended on the size of his family and two of Sechele's five wives were the daughters of under-chiefs who had helped him come to power. Now Sechele announced that he would give each wife a present of new clothes and send them back to their parents or families.

The villagers were horrified by the news. No work was done that day. The women did not go out and tend their crops, but stayed in their huts. The men looked downcast and a large group gathered in the meeting place and spoke angrily against the chief.

Livingstone visited the wives. He was particularly fond of two of the younger wives, Makhari and Mokokon, who during his visits to Sechele's family had been his most receptive pupils. Both wives were very distraught. Livingstone found Makhari in tears. She gave him back his Bible which, she said in a choking voice, would no longer be of any use to her now that she had to leave the village and go where there was no word of God. Mokokon was also crying, but as she had a young daughter and no family to return to, she was allowed to remain at Kolobeng.

As the day of Sechele's baptism approached, the atmosphere in the village worsened. Dark mutterings followed Livingstone round the village, and one of the elders even remarked that it was a shame that the lion at Mabotsa hadn't finished him off after all. However, the Africans mostly reserved their curses for their chief, who they felt was deserting his people and becoming a white man's plaything.

In October 1848 Chief Sechele, dressed in a long cloak made for him in Scotland and sitting on a chair donated by a group of religious ladies from Birmingham, entered into the fellowship of Jesus and took his first Holy Communion. Sechele's baptism should have been a joyous occasion for Livingstone – his very first convert and a chief at that! But the villagers, who all gathered round for the ceremony, rocked on their haunches and wept and wailed as if this were a funeral. And when Livingstone picked up the little metal bowl of water and anointed Sechele's head, the crowd gasped with horror, for they believed that their chief was about to drink a dead man's brains.

Afterwards, when the crowd were still dubiously inspecting the little metal bowl and sniffing the liquid inside, a village elder with tears coursing down his cheeks turned to Livingstone and said bitterly, 'You could at least have waited until we got rain.'

The rains didn't come. Day after day, the villagers pleaded with Livingstone to let Sechele make rain. Christmas passed and the New Year began, and on the plains by Kolobeng the haunches of the cattle jutted out and the cracks in the ground grew deeper, and still there was no rain.

At night Livingstone lay awake while his wife Mary, now fat and heavy with their third child, snuffled and snored. Oh, he was so bored! And what good was he doing here? It was true that Sechele was doing well – he had even started learning English and was thrilled with his new christening present: a Toby-jug with the Duke of Wellington's head on it. And even dear little Mokokon, who had been so upset when Sechele had to abandon her, seemed more cheerful these days. He had noticed she had put on weight recently and was even getting a little puffy round the cheeks.

But what about the rest of the village? Where were they on Sundays? Every week fewer and fewer villagers came to the church services. Attendance at Mary's little primary school was also slumping. And when Livingstone rebuked the villagers for not listening to the word of God, they asked him what good to them was a God that didn't bring rain? For *still* the skies remained dry. Was God just mocking him?

Livingstone couldn't bear to lie in bed any longer. He got to his feet and pulled back the buffalo skin over the front door. Moving very carefully in case of snakes, he stepped out into the darkness. A hot dry wind hit his face. Above him the night sky was bright with stars and pitilessly clear. There were no clouds, and, it seemed, no hope of rain.

He muttered to himself, 'Oh Satan, prince of the power of the air, art thou hindering us?'

In the far-off hills a wolf howled.

CHAPTER FOUR

Five months after Sechele's conversion, Livingstone discovered that Mokokon was pregnant. Nobody in the village needed to count on their fingers to work out that this meant the chief had be sleeping with his wife long after he had supposedly renounced polygamy*. Fancy clothes and Toby-jugs had not done the trick – Livingstone's one and only convert had returned to his old ways.

The relapse of Sechele marked the beginning of the end of Livingstone's days as a missionary. He would continue to think of himself as specially chosen – God had sent him to Africa with a particular purpose – but he now began to turn his attention to exploration.

In the summer of 1849 Livingstone went north, crossing the great Kalahari desert with the big game hunter

William Cotton Oswell. The men were searching for Lake Ngami, which, it was thought, had never been seen by a European.

After two months they came to the shores of the lake, but could go no further as the local tribal chief refused to allow them to cross. Eventually Oswell and Livingstone, having decided to return the following year with their own collapsible boat, turned back.

But the following year Livingstone didn't wait for Oswell. Instead he set out with his family, even though Mary was five months pregnant and the children were tiny – Robert was four, Agnes three and baby Thomas just one. The wagon trundled slowly through the blinding heat of the desert, the wheels sinking continually in the sand. When the Livingstones reached the River Zouga, the oxen were bitten by tsetse fly and started to die. But the party struggled on. It was a difficult journey – at one point the wagon fell down a covered pit that the local tribesmen had constructed to trap game – but at last they reached the banks of Lake Ngami.

Here the children, now covered from head to toe with insect bites, came down with malaria. Livingstone, who dosed them with quinine* till their ears rang, was most interested to note how the disease affected his children differently. Agnes's fever would disappear completely and then re-occur maybe a day later, whereas Baby Thomas remained continually ill, with the sickness periodically waxing and waning. Malaria was fascinating! If only he had his own hospital to study the effects better.

And if only he could go on, over the lake into the uncharted lands beyond. He would show that central Africa was a fertile, well-watered land, not the endless desert that the white men supposed it to be! He would write up his findings for the London Missionary Society and the Royal Geographical Society. He would open up Central Africa for 'The Three Cs' that were to become his motto: Christianity, Civilisation and Commerce.

But he couldn't go on now. Not with the children so weak – Agnes and Thomas could no longer stand up on their own. And Mary Livingstone was nearing her confinement. So, with great regret, Livingstone turned back and started the long, hot trek back across 200 miles of desert – days and days of joggling slowly along in the blinding heat, with poor food and sometimes not a drop to drink.

A week after the Livingstones arrived back in Kolobeng, Mary gave birth to her fourth child, a blue-eyed baby girl called Elizabeth. But the strain had been too much. Mary Livingstone soon fell ill and for two months remained paralysed down one side of her face and body. Meanwhile the Livingstone children all came down with a chest infection. Robert, who very nearly died, finally pulled through. But the new baby hovered on the brink for four days and finally opened her eyes, let out a scream and died.

For years Livingstone was haunted by Baby Elizabeth's final scream, but it didn't put him off his plans. A year later, in April 1851, he and his family set out once more to cross the Kalahari desert, and yet again Mary Livingstone was heavily pregnant.

Fortunately this time Oswell was accompanying them, and he went ahead trying to find water. But it had been an exceptionally dry summer and many of the wells were dry. At one point, they spent five days without water and Livingstone feared that his children would perish before his eyes – they were now bug-eyed, their lips were swollen and their tongues black with thirst. But at last they came to a small stagnant pool with clumps of rhinoceros dung floating on the surface. As the flies buzzed around them, they all knelt and happily gulped down the putrid water.

The Livingstones' wagons rumbled slowly on up through the Kalahari, into the lands of the Ngami and finally came to stop on the banks of the River Chobe. They were now in the country of the warlike Makololo tribe, and their majestic, bloodthirsty chief Sebitoane.

Sebitoane needed guns and was delighted to meet the white men. On their first evening, he sat round their fire with them and talked through the night. As the burning wood flickered its light on the reeds around them, Sebitoane told of great battles lost and won, of wondrous feats of daring, of subtle strategies, of savage vengeance, of great moments of generosity to van-quished foes. Sebitoane spoke too of the visits of the neighbouring Mambari tribe, who came with clothes and guns and bolts of cloth. The Mambari would not exchange their goods for cattle. Instead they wanted people – young boys in particular, whom they could then sell on to the Portuguese traders as slaves.

The Makololo had succumbed to the temptation and raided other tribes to kidnap slaves. In the days that followed, Livingstone and Oswell noted more and more European goods among the Makololo. One of Sebitoane's braves, a great iron ramrod of a man, walked around proudly dressed in a lady's negligée which barely came to his knees. He told Livingstone that he had bartered a woman to get this fine item of clothing. Again and again, they heard the same story: of goods being traded for people. Behind every gun or dressing-gown lay a fearful tale of slavery and suffering.

Just three weeks after Livingstone and Oswell's arrival, Sebitoane suddenly fell ill and died of pneumonia. The following day the chief was buried in his cattle pen, with the cows driven back and forth over the plot to obliterate any traces on the ground, and so prevent witches disinterring the body. As the cattle stampeded back and forth, Livingstone sat in his camp and pondered gloomily. Sebitioane had been Livingstone's favourite tribal chief, and yet now the poor man's soul would be consigned to everlasting darkness.

But Livingstone was still intent on exploring the region. He and Oswell had heard there was a great river 100 miles to the north and eventually they resumed their journey, leaving Mary Livingstone and the children back at their camp with the wagons. After several days the two men made their way through some marshy land and came out on the banks of a huge, fast-flowing river so wide that the trees on the far bank seemed just tiny specks.

A sinewy old man agreed to take Livingstone and Oswell out on to the river in his canoe. It was a wobbly, uncomfortable journey. The current was very fast and the canoe lurched from side to side. But the old man paddled nimbly and soon they were in the very middle of the river.

Livingstone, perched with his knees almost up to his chin, gawped at the dark water parting so fast on either side of the canoe. He couldn't swim, but it never occurred to him to be scared. Instead other thoughts flowed through his mind, even faster than the river around him: He, David Livingstone, was the first white man to find this mighty river! This river – which must surely be the upper part of the Zambesi which flowed eastward and out into the Indian Ocean at Mozambique – was the future! This river would be the highway into Africa! No more need for dangerous desert crossings. No more hacking paths through the jungle. One day this river would take steamboats, and the steamboats would be filled with traders and missionaries. And the traders would put an end to the evil slave trade – for instead of trading in people, the Makololo would be able to sell ivory and palm oil, ostrich feathers and wax. Maybe they would even find gold. And it would all be thanks to the mighty river, and thanks to David Livingstone, the first white man to discover it and open up the heart of Africa to Christianity, Civilisation and Commerce.

Livingstone, overwhelmed by the grandeur of his emotions, felt tears brimming in his eyes. But when he looked up, he realised that the old man was watching him intently. A terrible thought struck him: maybe the old fellow thought he was scared of alligators? Livingstone quickly looked away and, in order to regain his composure, turned his mind to other things. He thought hard about the geological formation of southern Africa and the migratory habits of springboks* and the stupidity of gnus* and – how could he ever forget? – the dreadful state of his bowels. His tears dried up instantly.

***

Livingstone and Oswell returned south and, on the banks of the River Zouga, Mary Livingstone gave birth to her fifth child, a little boy, who was christened William Oswell, in honour of the family's travelling companion. After the birth Mary Livingstone was again paralysed down one side of her body, but she did eventually recover and the family made their way slowly back across the Kalahari desert. Then, after a short stopover at Kolobeng, they went on down to Cape Town. Livingstone had set his heart on exploring central Africa and had decided that he must send his family back to Britain.

What a sight the Livingstones were when their wagon first trundled into Cape Town! Livingstone's black coat was 12 years old – shiny and threadbare. Mrs Livingstone, whose figure had thickened with childbirth, was squeezing out of a dress many inches too small. The children were barefoot and dressed in rags.

The Livingstones stayed in Cape Town where, thanks to a gift of £200 from Oswell, everyone was fitted out in new clothes. The children found this new town life bizarre. They had never seen a horse-drawn carriage or a shop; they had never used a candle snuffer or sucked a lemon drop. They had never worn so many clothes before. So much prickly flannel! And the hatefully tight button-up boots! Even Livingstone had trouble adjusting – for several days he could only come down staircases backwards as if descending a ladder.

When the day finally came for their ship to set sail, Livingstone looked at his children standing on the quay-side with their new capes and their straight partings. For a moment he thought they looked almost respectable. But then he looked a little closer. Robert, who was seven and assumed all footwear was interchangeable, had his boots on the wrong way round again. Agnes, despite the new bonnet, was still shamefully sun-tanned. And little Thomas in his multitude of new petticoats did wriggle so! A three-year-old should surely know better!

Livingstone gave a gruff little cough. He thought it appropriate to mark his family's departure with a short, improving speech. But his throat was still sore from an operation to remove his uvula. He had hoped that this might improve his rather muffled speech, but he still sounded as if he was speaking with a pebble in his mouth. 'Children,' said Livingstone. 'It will be two years before you see me next, perhaps longer. So from now onwards you are to think of Jesus as your father. I have given you back to him and you are in his care. Obey him at all times! He will be watching.'

Livingstone eyed Robert sternly. His seven-year-old son was excessively obstinate and, so far, regular thrashing had done no good. Now the wretched child's lower lip was sticking out. Was it more wilfulness, or a display of sentiment? In either case it showed weakness of character.

Livingstone loomed over the child, 'Robert, my man!'

'Father, when will we return to Kolobeng?' asked Robert miserably.

'Never!' Livingstone gave another gruff cough. 'You are the children of a missionary. For you God has chosen the bread of adversity and the waters of affliction.'

Then, with a quick kiss on the cheek to his wife, and a tap on the head to each of his children, Livingstone dismissed his family. As they walked towards the ship, he called out, 'Single file up the gangway and remember your prayers.'

They were not to see him again for five years.

CHAPTER FIVE

Livingstone travelled north again and finally in the spring of 1853, after wading for two days through waist-deep swamp and crossing the River Chobe, he arrived in the Makololo town of Linyanti. The tribesmen, who said no one had ever crossed the swamp before, helped him bring his men and wagons round by an easier route.

Livingstone brought the Makololo vast quantities of gifts including 100lbs of lead, 20lbs of tin, plenty of gunpowder, three goats to improve local stock, two cats, some hens, two great coils of brass wire, an umbrella, a candlestick, a powder horn, a frying-pan and a leaking pot. Chief Sekeletu, Sebituane's 18-year-old son, was thrilled and offered him men to accompany him on his travels.

Livingstone took him up on this offer and the two men, accompanied by a fleet of 33 canoes, went on a journey. They paddled 300 miles north, up the Zambesi river to the Barotse valley in search of a healthy site where Livingstone would one day be able to build a missionary station. But he soon concluded that there was malaria everywhere. He had contracted the disease himself, and day after day he lay at the bottom of his canoe shivering with fever, desperate to urinate, with his stomach and head in agony and his face covered in boils.

Meanwhile, over his prostrate body, the Makololo would talk loudly among themselves, reliving old battles and imitating the death throes of their victims. Normally they laughed uproariously as they did so, but sometimes the arguments about head counts grew vicious:

'You've only killed 27 braves!'

'No I haven't! Thirty-three is my number. And only yesterday I hacked up Mpepe's uncle and fed him in bits to the alligators.'

'That was an execution. He was old and unarmed. Doesn't count.'

'Yes it does, and give me the hashish pipe. You've

been coughing like an old gibbon.'

'No!'

'Give it to me or I'll smash your head in with this paddle.'

'No it's mine!'

'It's mine!'

And so on. How Livingstone loathed them. How he wished he was back with Sechele and the Bakwains.

***

In November 1853, Livingstone started on his first great journey, compared with which all his previous travels over the Kalahari desert would seem like brief forays. Now he was to make his way over one thousand miles north-west across central Africa to the Portuguese coastal trading post of Luanda, in what is today Angola.

For the journey Chief Sekeletu lent Livingstone 27 men, but only two of them were Makololo, the rest came from subject tribes. Sekeletu also gave Livingstone several riding oxen, as much food as he could carry, and ivory, some of which was a gift and some of which he was to trade with on the chief's behalf.

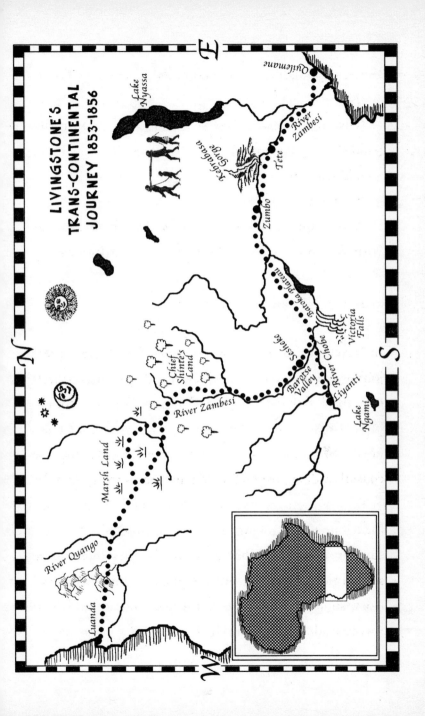

Livingstone travelled light. For his own comfort he had only a small leaky tent, a sheepskin blanket and a rug. He knew that his supply of beads, cloth and wire would not be enough to pay for food and passage during the journey. But he did not stint on his scientific equipment. He had a thermometer, a sextant*, a telescope, a chronometer*, an artificial horizon, and a pair of compasses. Livingstone was determined to chart his way as accurately as possible, and made detailed maps and recordings throughout the trip.

In addition, Livingstone took four tin boxes, each about 40 centimetres square. One box was filled with tidy clothes – a spare shirt, trousers and shoes for the far-off day when he would return to civilisation. Another box was for medicines – though much of this was stolen before he left, and throughout the trip he would be dangerously short of quinine, which at that time was the only drug which could effectively relieve the symptoms of malaria. A third box contained Livingstone's books, including a nautical almanac, a set of logarithm tables and a Bible. And the fourth box held his 'magic lantern', a heavy device made of mahogany and tin, with a spirit lamp and a refracting mirror inside, and a huge brass lens on the front. The magic lantern was in essence a primitive form of film projector with painted glass slides and a little lever attached which allowed the figures to move back and forth. Livingstone became a dab hand at these performances, and at night he would get his men to hang a large piece of cloth from two branches and he would tell Old Testament Bible stories. The Makololo were particularly fond of his dramatic 'Parting of the Red Sea'. And he did a wonderfully tempestuous 'Trials of Job'.

This was hardly surprising, for at the time Livingstone's life had much in common with the biblical figure: like Job, Livingstone was wracked with pain, and like Job, he was plagued with sores.

All that year, Livingstone had battled with illness, and had had eight outbreaks of malarial fever. So by November, he was weak and thin. He suffered from giddiness whenever he looked up and was also having trouble with his bowels: his stools were bloody and only produced with the greatest discomfort. He recorded these problems in his diary.

But – like Job – Livingstone was persistent. And nothing whatsoever would deter him from his journey across

Africa. So, on 11th November 1853, Livingstone bade farewell to Sekeletu and set out on his way down the winding Chobe river. A week later he came out on to the Zambesi.

And again he was struck by the beauty and grandeur of the river. This great tranquil expanse of water was sometimes a mile wide, with small islands dotted in its midst, and a vast cloudless sky arching overhead. The banks were lined with trees: the towering palmyras, the date palms with their delicate bright green fronds, the dark motsouri trees covered in tiny pink plums.

The days on the river slid by. Sometimes Livingstone lay in the bottom of the canoe shivering with fever, and only getting up to vomit over the side. But when he felt a little better, he would prop himself up on his elbows and watch.

Livingstone followed the birds closely. Soon he could recognise the harsh scream of the ibis and the metallic 'tinc tinc tinc' sound of the hammering iron bird (*Pluvianus armatus* or the 'setula-tsipi'). He loved to see the pretty scissorbills skimming the surface of the water with their beaks scooping up insects, and he marvelled at how the fierce fish-hawks repeatedly stole catches from the great purse-like bills of the stupid pelicans.

Hippos lolled in the river, blowing out great spurts of water and gallumphing about in the mud. Livingstone noticed how, in the middle of the river, the very young baby hippos would stand on their mothers' backs and the mothers, knowing that the babies needed to draw breath more often, would come up for air more quickly than usual. He also became accustomed to the dull thud of an alligator plunging into the water as they came round a corner. And he saw how the iguanas, which sunned themselves on the overhanging branches, would drop into the water as Livingstone's canoes approached. They were wise – for the boatman considered their soft glutinous flesh to be a delicacy and were always ready with their spears. Livingstone wasn't so sure about broiled* iguana – the meat had a disagreeable way of slithering around in the mouth.

All this – and much, much more – he recorded in his diaries. Every night, when his men and his oxen lay huddled asleep on the ground and all that could be heard was the croaking of frogs and the occasional cry of the hyena, Livingstone would sit writing his journals by the light of the fire.

He would describe the plants, the fish, the birds. He would note changes in vegetation, record temperatures, examine the anatomy of dead animals. He wanted to know *everything*. He could barely pass a tree stump without counting the rings in the wood.

And he was *so* hardworking: even if the journey had been harsh that day, even if they had to carry the canoes over rapids and he had spent an age crouched straining behind a tree with his insides in knots, he would still make meticulous notes. And although he was still suffering from dizziness and every time he looked into the sky the world seemed to lurch on its bearings, he never failed to get out his sextant and chronometer, and map out exactly where he was.

At five in the morning, after only a few hours sleep, Livingstone and his men would rise. While the men loaded the canoes, Livingstone would dress and drink his coffee. Then, in the cool of the early morning, they would embark. These first two hours of the journey were the best, when the men would paddle most vigorously. Then things would begin to slacken. At 11 o'clock they would all stop, land, and eat any meat left over from the night before, or have a biscuit with honey.

After an hour's rest they would return to the water, with everyone cowering under umbrellas to keep away from the heat.

Two hours before sunset they would make their camp. Livingstone's men would collect grass to make a bed for him and set some poles in the ground on which to erect his tent. Supper was a drink of coffee, another biscuit, or some coarse bread made from maize meal and anything they had been lucky enough to kill that day. The method of cooking was always the same: the men cut the meat into thin strips, put it in a pot and covered it with water. When the pot boiled itself dry, the meat was considered ready.

Every man had his allotted place and role. The 'herald' collected the wood for the fire and in return was rewarded with the head of any creature that they killed. The two Makololo men always ate on Livingstone's left- and right-hand sides and at night they would sleep on either side of his tent. The others would sleep in groups round the fire according to their tribe.

***

By the end of 1853, the landscape had opened out into parkland and Livingstone was delighted to find himself surrounded by meadows and ponds and clusters of tall straight trees. But the Zambesi had become much narrower and would soon be impassable in the canoes. Livingstone was now in the land of the Balonda people who insisted he abandon the river and travel overland to visit their leader, Great Chief Shinte.

The journey took several days. Shinte's indomitable niece Manenko, jingling with iron anklets and covered from head to foot in glistening ox fat and red ochre, strode out ahead, while her drummer kept up a continuous beat. Behind came Livingstone, riding on Sinbad, his bad-tempered ox. Livingstone was now having a particularly bad attack of malaria, and kept sliding off Sinbad's back. The ox never lost an opportunity to give him a sharp kick, or tread on his fingers.

On the second day, Manenko led the expedition into a forest so thick that the travellers had to hew their way through with axes. The rain thundered down and, as they travelled north, the forest became even denser and darker. All around grew huge white mushrooms as big as the crown of a man's hat, and vast trees stood with creepers the size of boa constrictors wrapped round and round their trunks.

The rains poured down into the dim, shut-in green world that the explorers now inhabited. All day long Livingstone's soaking clothes stuck to his body, and at night he watched miserably as the rainwater splashed into his foul manioc* gruel. However, he found that the giant mushrooms were delicious.

After a week's walking, they came down into Shinte's valley. Here, outside the village, they waited an extra day in the rain while Manenko sent a herald to forewarn of their arrival. Eventually, when the sun was thought to be high enough to make a lucky entrance, Livingstone led his men into the town.

Immediately a rabble of tribesmen waving guns in the air ran at them. Livingstone and his men waited. The rabble surrounded them and then simply stood and stared. Livingstone kept a solemn expression, even though he did notice that most of the tribesmen had no notion how to use a firearm and were holding their guns by the barrel. After an hour the Balonda got bored of glowering and gradually dispersed, leaving Livingstone and his followers free to set up camp.

Shinte's reception was held the following morning. A thousand Balonda, all armed and decorated, trooped into the enormous meeting space in the centre of the village. Livingstone found an unoccupied tree and he and his men sat down beside it in a group. At the far end of the meeting place, under the shade of a vast banian tree, Great Chief Shinte presided. The chief, dressed in a scarlet kilt and a profusion of bright beads and bracelets, looked in his mid-fifties. Under his magnificent helmet of goose feathers was a lined face with tired, sunken eyes.

Shinte had many, many wives. Behind him sat about a hundred women all dressed in bright red baize*, like a shoal of tropical fish. The chief wife was positioned a little forward from the rest and wore a strange red cap.

The ceremonies seemed interminable. Each section of the Balonda tribe came forward in turn to proclaim their allegiance to the chief. Then the men gave dances of tribute and – as a mark of respect – rubbed their chests and arms with ash. Afterwards came more displays of strength, and more dances, and more running to and fro with javelins and shields. This continued for hours: the people clapped their hands and the musicians beat their marimbas and the court toadies spouted praise and the braves sweated into their anklets and the drums beat on and on and on.

The shoal of wives swayed with the drumbeats and at intervals they would break into song. But Great Chief Shinte remained very still on his leopard-skin throne and never took his old oyster eyes off Livingstone.

Livingstone stared calmly back. He suspected that the chief hadn't seen a white man like him before. He knew his Makololo porters had told the Balonda that the white man came from the sea. They had explained that the strange wig of lion's mane on the white man's head wasn't a wig at all. It was *real*. It was *hair*. Livingstone must surely have come from the sea – that was why his hair was so straight, just like their hair was when they dipped their head in water. Livingstone was really a sort of merman.

Shinte was watchful that first day, but later he grew to like his strange merman. Every couple of days he would invite him to his palace, which looked like a giant basket and was constructed from tall poles with weeds woven through them, and there the two men would sit drinking beer, conversing slowly with the help of an interpreter.

Shinte gave his visitor corn and manioc and hens. Livingstone reciprocated with beads and sermons and calabashes* of clarified butter.

Finally, when Livingstone had recovered his strength after yet another outbreak of malaria, he put on a show with his magic lantern. The performance wasn't a great success. When he came to the scene where Abraham raises his knife to kill his son Isaac, Shinte's wives screamed and scurried off in a flurry of red baize and hid among their banana plantations. No amount of reassurance that this was all make-believe would bring them back.

One day, Livingstone arrived at Shinte's reed palace to find that the chief had a quite different gift from usual. Standing beside the throne was a girl of about ten years old. The girl, who was carefully oiled and ochred, kept her eyes fixed on the ground. Her legs were trembling.

Livingstone's heart gave a little flutter of horror, but he kept his face impassive and gave a deferential bow.

'She will bring you your water,' declared Shinte. 'A great man must always have a child.'

Livingstone bowed again. Shinte gave the girl a pat on the rump.

'She is healthy and well fed.'

'She is indeed, oh honourable chief. But I regret I cannot take her,' replied Livingstone.

But Shinte's interpreter said nothing.

Livingstone thought of his own daughter. Agnes would be nearly seven now. He tried again. 'Tell him I cannot take her.'

The interpreter looked at him aghast.

'I have four children of my own,' added Livingstone. 'Tell the most honourable chief I would be most worried should my chief take my little girl and give her away. I would prefer it if this girl remained here to carry water for her own mother.'

The interpreter spoke to Shinte. The chief's eyes clouded with anger and he spoke abruptly to the courtier, who took the girl away. Then Shinte turned back to Livingstone, and gave him a pointy little grin.

Livingstone smiled back. It was curious, he thought, how filed teeth always did look so grey. Was it the damage to the enamel? Or something they ate?

Livingstone and Shinte were still slowly sipping their beer when the courtier returned. He did not come empty handed. He led in *another* girl. She was older – a head taller than her predecessor – and had small, budding breasts.

Livingstone, flushing from the neck up, repeated what he had said earlier about not wishing to take a child away from its mother.

Shinte protested. This girl was almost a woman. She would soon be able to bear him a fine son…

But Livingstone quickly finished his beer, thanked Shinte for his hospitality and bade him farewell. He had already started to bow his way backwards out of the room when a small fat soothsayer grabbed his arm; as usual, it was a request for gifts.

'The chief's mouth is bitter from want of beef,' said the soothsayer thickly.

Great Chief Shinte gave his visitor a most hopeful smile.

As Livingstone returned to his bowing, he said to himself that it was time to be on his way again. He still had 600 miles to go before he reached the coast.

***

In late January 1854, Livingstone set off back into the

forest. Again the heavy rains came, and soon all the guns and surgical instruments were rusty and Livingstone's rotten, tattered little tent smelt like an old dog. Day after day they trudged on. Now Livingstone was no longer scanning the surroundings with his gun at the ready, for there was little game in the forest. Instead the men had to make do with the occasional mouse. Once they also caught a bizarre-looking, pale blue mole and ate it with relish.

As Livingstone went west, the corrupting effects of the slave trade became more marked and he noticed that the people were less and less friendly. The normal African traditions of hospitality to travellers had gone, and now food was not willingly offered but had to be bought. The local tribes also demanded 'hongo' or payment for passing through territory. If there were a river to cross, they would ask for still more hongo. At one river Livingstone ended up paying hongo three times: once before crossing, again when half his men were on the far bank and a third time just before he and the last of his men embarked.

Livingstone could ill afford the payments. He was running out of beads and cloth and had very little food.

But there were still a few spare oxen and when they killed one they cut the hide into two-inch strips. The leather was very popular for making girdles, and they sold each strip for meal or manioc.

In early March, Livingstone and his men, holding on to the tails of their oxen, forded their way through a series of flooded valleys and entered the territory of the Chiboque tribe. The Chiboque were particularly hostile, and one day Livingstone and his men found that their encampment was surrounded by angry warriors brandishing swords and pointing their guns at the white man. Livingstone sat on his camp stool with his double-barrelled gun across his knees and talked calmly. When a young Chiboque charged him from behind, Livingstone swivelled round and thrust the muzzle at his mouth and the man backed off. Meanwhile, some of Livingstone's men had crept round behind the chief and his headman and now threatened them with spears. Eventually the Chiboque retreated, but only after Livingstone had given them one of his precious oxen. The Chiboque had promised to reciprocate with gifts. Later they brought Livingstone a small basket of meal and a couple of pounds of meat from his own ox.

Livingstone and his men travelled on through the heavy rains. Things were getting worse. Guides led them astray, food was scarce and the dark forests weighed on everybody's spirits. Livingstone's fever had returned, his bottom was covered in saddle-sores and he was now so weak that he was falling off Sinbad three or four times a day.

He noticed that his men were becoming less prompt at helping him back on to the ox. They stopped looking him in the eye, they dawdled on the path, they muttered in twos and threes, they took forever to build the nightly stockade. Once or twice he even had to ask them to make his coffee. Livingstone knew the men were beginning to doubt him.

Then one night, after they had finished their miserable portions of gruel, one of the Makololo blurted out, 'The big water is only a white man's story!'

Glaring at the man, Livingstone threw down his almanac and rose to his feet. He stood with his back to the fire, his legs splayed and his jaw clenched. Livingstone waited until an uneasy silence fell on the group. Then he declared, 'You are all my men and we stick together. I tell you now that I am a man of God and not a slave trader. This you know full well. And I will hear no more about the sea being an invention. The sea is real!'

He took out his pistol and raised it in the air.

'And *this* I will use against any man who dares repeat such infamous lies!'

Livingstone furrowed his brow and scowled ferociously at the bowed heads in front of him. He looked magnificent when he was angry, especially now with the steam from his sodden breeches rising up behind him.

***

In March 1854, Livingstone and his men finally came out of the forest and found themselves in a bright, sunny clearing on the edge a steep cliff. A thousand feet below them was the valley of the River Quango, and in the far distance, beyond more forests and plains, lay the peaks of the Tala Mungongo mountains, which they would have to cross before reaching the coast.

The descent into the valley was steep and Livingstone was now so weak from fever that his men had to lead him down the path. The land below turned out to be scraggy woodland with bamboo as thick as a man's arm.

Livingstone and his men trudged on. The local Bashinje tribe would not give them manioc or meal. And now that Livingstone's razors, spoons, beads and cloth had all gone, and he had only the clothes he stood up in, there was almost nothing left for them to trade with.

After four days, Livingstone and his men reached the banks of the River Quango. They were in the middle of a bitter argument with a Bashinje chief who was demanding a man as hongo, when a young Portuguese sergeant of the militia appeared and helped them cross the river into Portuguese controlled territory.

That night Livingstone and his men camped in the sergeant's military base. For five days they remained there. Livingstone breakfasted on peanuts, roasted maize, guavas and honey. He dined on chicken and beef. By the time, he and his men set off again, the sergeant's vegetable garden was looking decidedly bare.

They travelled on, making good progress, and on 24th April they reached the foot of the Tala Mungongo mountain ridge. The next morning they climbed the ascent and Livingstone spent that night in a little wattle and daub hut rife with fleas. Then they went on through the forest and meadows of the high plateaux. By the first week of May, Livingstone and his men had covered 200 miles and reached the settlement of Ambaca, which was only 150 miles from the coast.

But, as they left Ambaca and made the final lap of the journey down from the mountains onto the coastal plain, Livingstone's health began to crack. The bouts of malaria, which had wracked him throughout the journey, now became one long, continuous fever and he woke every morning to find his bedclothes dripping in sweat. Livingstone's dysentery also reached a climax of awfulness. His guts felt as though they were being squeezed through a mangle. His mind had become numb and fumbling – he could not even remember the days of the week or the names of his men. In fact all of him – his heart, his lungs, his innards – seemed to be on the verge of collapse. Only his saddle-sores were flourishing – they had spread out, colonising his thighs and the cracks in his groin.

By the time they came close to Luanda the men had to carry Livingstone on a makeshift stretcher, where he lay sweating like a bullfrog and sinking further and further into delirium.

And so things remained until, on a fine morning in late May as the party were trudging across the plains, one of the men shouted, 'Look! Look! Look up ahead!' But Livingstone just groaned, and he didn't see the faint glimmer of a thin blue line up on the horizon.

Later, as they walked on through the midday sun, the thin blue line gradually thickened into a long bright ribbon and finally in the afternoon the men mounted the brow of a small hill and saw the glorious, glimmering Atlantic Ocean stretched out before them like a silken cloth.

The men crouched down on their heels, screwed their eyes up and stared out over the water in mute astonishment. These tribesmen from central Africa had always thought the world was one huge, limitless plain, but here was the proof that things were very different, and very strange. And this great expanse of salt water was a new element to them. They could smell for the first time the briny, brackish smells of the sea and they could hear for the first time the sounds of the sea; the breaking of the waves and the screech of the seabirds overhead.

The first man to break the silence shuddered as he spoke. His voice was low, almost a whisper: 'We marched along with our fathers, we believed what the ancients always told us was true, that the world has no end. But all at once the world says to us, 'I am finished; there is no more of me!'

The man looked down the hill to where the land fell away. Underneath lay the shore where the tide pulled and sucked on the tiny pebbles.

The man clasped his arms round his knees. At least the ground here under his feet was steady. He wasn't sure he liked the edge of the world.

CHAPTER SIX

L ivingstone was mortally ill when he was carried into
Luanda, but within a few weeks he had gained
enough strength to start organising his next venture. It
was now clear to him that the route he'd taken from central Africa to the west coast would never provide good
access for trade. It was simply too difficult: too many
waist-high swamps, too many hostile tribes, too many
obstacles of every kind. Even to have survived the journey – and to have brought all his men through alive –
was an accomplishment.

So, he decided, another way had to be found to open
up central Africa to trade and missionaries. This time he
would travel east. He would go back across the continent, through Linyanti and on to the east coast of Africa
in Mozambique. And so, at the beginning of 1855, he set

off again, retracing his steps for 1,200 miles. He went back over the plains and the mountains and through the waist-high swamps and the hot, dank forests.

Again he had his customary toll of misfortunes: he was attacked by the Chiboque, and he lost the sight of one eye by walking into a jutting-out branch. His hearing started to fail from repeated doses of quinine, and he acquired a fresh symptom – he started to vomit blood. Sinbad the bad-tempered ox died. And at the Zambesi river Livingstone's canoe was almost overturned by an enraged female hippo whose young had been killed the day before.

But, after nine months, Livingstone reached Linyanti, where Sekeletu greeted him warmly and supplied him, for the second leg of the journey, with a new, larger retinue of men and another mass of ivory to sell on his behalf.

In return, Livingstone was to do a little shopping for the chief when he reached the coast. Sekeletu's list was long – he wanted arms and cloth, but also an iron rocking-chair and a pair of spectacles with green glass.

And so Livingstone set off again down the Zambesi and a month later he came to the great falls of

Mosioatunya. Livingstone approached by canoe, and five or six miles before he arrived he saw huge white columns of spray rising up like smoke into the sky.

Livingstone's guide brought the canoe down the rapids to an island in the middle of the river. From here he looked out over the very edge of the cataract*, where an enormous curtain of water a mile long crashed down into a rocky canyon far below. The roar of the water was deafening.

Livingstone jotted down measurements, carved his initials and the date – 1855 – in a nearby tree. Then, being the 19th-century explorer that he was, he took another white man's prerogative and, renamed the waterfall. The African name 'Mosioatunya' meant 'the falls of thundering smoke', and evoked the sound and sight of this magnificent cataract. Livingstone, however, decided to rename it 'The Victoria Falls' in honour of his queen, who had never set foot in Africa.

***

Afterwards Livingstone left the banks of the Zambesi and, cutting across a great loop in the river, went north up on to the rolling hills of the Batoka plateau. Here all around him stretched miles and miles of rich pastureland dotted with huge fruit trees and corn poppies and thousands of tiny white flowers. The tips of the hills had outcrops of marble that shone in the sunlight.

Livingstone looked down into valleys filled with more wild animals than he had ever seen in all his years in Africa: buffaloes, elands, hartebeest, gnus, elephants. The birds and beasts were so wonderfully tame! He shot four geese with just two bullets! There were even – such a nice touch for a homesick Scot – little crickets that made a noise like the drone of a bagpipe

Livingstone breathed in the cool, crisp air. Thanks to the fact that he had acquired some wheat flour and been able to add bread to his diet, his bowels now felt tiptop and regular. He was suffused with a sense of wellbeing and optimism.

What better place than the Batoka plateau! Here there was no tsetse fly, no malaria, no rainstorms. The soil was fertile, the conditions suited cattle, and might prove excellent for sheep. A perfect paradise! Finally he had found an ideal spot for his new missionary and trading settlement. Here the new colony would start cleansing Africa of slavery and barbarism!

There was of course the small matter of communication with the outside world: the Batoka plateau was still more than 800 miles from the east coast of Africa. But as long as the Zambesi river proved navigable, that should prove no problem. A couple of sturdy steamers would do the trick.

And so, fired up with enthusiasm, Livingstone forged on ahead. In 1856 he came down off the plateau, and passed through the deserted Portuguese settlement of Zumbo where the soft sandstone houses were all melting back into the loam.

Crossing the Zumbo river, a tributary of the Zambesi, entailed a war of nerves. With hoards of armed Batoka tribesmen standing all around him, Livingstone and his men slowly crossed the river, using the one canoe that the local people had grudgingly lent them.

Livingstone had planned to follow the Zambesi all the way to the coast. But, shortly after leaving Zumbo, he decided to save a few miles and avoid some rough country, and he left the Zambesi and went inland, rejoining the river 200 miles downstream at the dilapidated Portuguese town of Tete.

This short cut meant that Livingstone never saw the Kebrabasa Falls, a 30-mile series of devastating cataracts that made the Zambesi completely impassable.

At Tete, Livingstone left most of his Makololo porters and travelled in a canoe for the last 270 miles to Quilemane, a town situated on the coast near to the mouth of the Zambesi river. This should have been the easiest part of the journey, but by now Livingstone was struck down by another bout of fever. Soon he was desperately ill and by the time he reached Quilemane he was close to death.

But again, just as he had at Luanda, Livingstone rallied. And within a few days of his arrival in Quilemane he had recovered sufficiently to start making arrangements for his return to England. He discovered that British warships had been calling in regularly at the town to enquire if he had arrived. The last warship, *HMS Frolic*, had sent in a rowing-boat, but the vessel had hit one of the many hidden sand bars in the mouth of the river and had capsized, drowning all eight members of the crew.

This news told Livingstone two important things.

Firstly, that he was now a very famous man – why otherwise would British Admiralty be sending out boats for him? And secondly, that terrible dangers lurked in the Zambesi river.

CHAPTER SEVEN

Livingstone came back to England to a hero's welcome. The Royal Geographical Society gave him a gold medal and he was granted the freedom of half a dozen major cities. He lunched with the Prime Minister Lord Palmerston and had tea (cream cakes, chocolate layer cake, cranberry tarts) with Queen Victoria in Buckingham Palace. Soon he was so well known that crowds of adoring fans mobbed him in Regent Street and a church service broke up in chaos with the congregation clambering over the pews to shake his hand.

Overall the attention was flattering. Various esteemed men of science with long sideburns heaped praise on him, and now he went out almost every night to dine with what he called 'the best society' and consumed fine wines, champagne and port.

With all his engagements, Livingstone was so busy he didn't see much of his family. When he arrived in England, it had been nearly five years since he had last seen his wife, and the children were like strangers to him. Those four and a half years of separation had been very difficult for Mary Livingstone who had arrived back in England with a family to support and very little money. And to the Livingstone children Britain had seemed an awful land – all coal smoke and corsets and people speaking English. Even in summer the climate was an endurance test.

At first the family had stayed with Livingstone's parents and two spinster sisters in their tiny cottage in Hamilton, outside Glasgow. But life in the cramped, chilly little cottage had proved intolerable, and within six months Mary Livingstone had argued with her parents-in-law and upped and left with her children. For the remaining years she had been constantly on the move, taking refuge with family friends, and staying in a succession of miserable boarding-houses with sour-faced landladies. In the winter of 1853, Mary Livingstone had suffered a nervous breakdown. She had recovered, but had started to drink heavily. During all this time there had been little news from her husband. And when he had sent a letter, the tone had tended to be stern and admonishing.

Livingstone's return to Britain did at least mean an end to his family's financial problems. In 1857 he published *Missionary Travels and Researches in South Africa*, a very detailed and upbeat account of his journeys. The book was an instant bestseller and made Livingstone rich.

Afterwards he did what so many successful authors do: he went on a lecture tour. Livingstone travelled up and down the country talking about the great future in store for Africa. The audiences loved him, for he was a passionate speaker and his weather-beaten face and his strangely muffled voice – he had acquired a way of speaking English as if it were a foreign language – only made him seem more exotic.

Livingstone talked of the potential for enormous cotton plantations on the Batoka plateau and called the Zambesi river an ideal waterway for shipping. He mentioned rich mineral resources in western Mozambique and enthused about the possibilities for growing sugar cane, wheat and coffee. He believed sincerely that by opening up Africa to his three 'C's – Civilisation, Commerce and Christianity – Britain would be able to replace the barbaric custom of slavery with more legitimate trade.

***

Very soon Livingstone was planning his next journey. This time he would bring a specially designed portable steamer, assemble it at the mouth of the Zambesi and travel upriver to the Batoka plateau accompanied by a team of experts. The aim was to see whether it would be possible to establish a missionary settlement in the area. The government gave him £5,000 (about £240,000 in today's money) towards the expedition and appointed him roving consul for the district of Quilemane on a salary of £500 a year. To celebrate his new title, Livingstone added a gold band to his navy-blue peaked cap.

To accompany him on the expedition were: Captain Norman Bedingfeld of the Royal Navy; Richard Thornton, a geologist; Dr John Kirk, a botanist and physician; Thomas Baines, the party's official artist;

Livingstone's younger brother Charles Livingstone, a non-conformist minister; and another Scot, the engineer George Rae. A few days after they left London, Livingstone gave a little speech in which he outlined their duties and also took the opportunity to urge the men to keep their bowels regular.

In May 1858, Livingstone and his team arrived at the mouth of the Zambesi aboard the *Pearl*. Because of the sand-bars in the estuary, it took two weeks before the captain found a way into the river. Even then the going was very difficult. Livingstone had hoped to travel as far as Tete, several hundred miles upriver, in the *Pearl*. But after just 40 miles the Zambesi became too shallow, and the ship had to turn back. George Rae bolted together the bits of the small, portable steamer which Livingstone had called *Ma Robert* – the Bakwain name for Mary Livingstone.

Ma Robert proved to be a nightmare. She was under-powered, her cylinders and boilers gave constant trouble and the steel hull was soon pitted with rust. Worse still, she consumed vast quantities of wood – it took a day and a half to chop the wood for one day's sailing – and was forever running aground on sandbanks. The tiny lit-

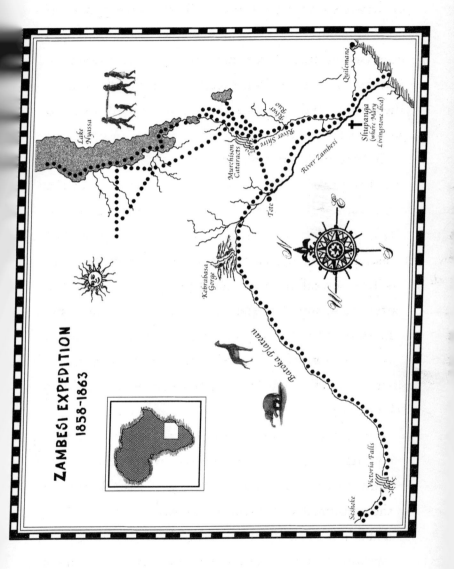

ZAMBESI EXPEDITION
1858-1863

Lake Nyassa

River Ruo

River Shire

Murchison Cataracts

Quilemane

Shupanga
(where Mary
Livingstone died)

River Zambesi

Tete

Kebrabasa
Gorge

Batoka Plateau

Victoria Falls

Seshcke

tle cabin was a boiling hell-hole. Arguments soon arose. Within two months Livingstone had fired his second-in-command, Captain Bedingfeld.

The party struggled on up the river, with the *Ma Robert* continually running aground in the sands and the men spending days sweating with winches and cables to get her afloat again.

In September, Livingstone finally reached Tete and was reunited with his Makololo porters who were delighted to see him again. But of 114 men left behind four years earlier, only 78 had survived. The area was not healthy, and at this point Thornton, Baines, and Charles Livingstone were all too ill to go on and had to remain at Tete.

But Livingstone continued upriver. His optimistic forecasts for central Africa and all that he had said in those impassioned lectures back in Britain hinged on the Zambesi being navigable as far as the Batoka plateau.

And, of course, it wasn't. On the second day out of Tete, the *Ma Robert* entered a valley with sheer black cliffs rising on either side. The river was now much narrower and the current became so strong that it buffeted the steamer against the rocks. Ahead lay a series of violent rapids. Livingstone and Kirk set off on foot over burning hot rocks. At first Livingstone clung to the belief that, somehow, *Ma Robert* would, given the right conditions, be able to sail through. But eventually, when he came face to face with a 30-foot waterfall – one of the biggest in the Kebrabasa gorge – even he had to concede defeat.

Instead of abandoning the expedition, Livingstone turned his attention to the Shire river, which joined the Zambesi further downstream, about 100 miles from the coast. Livingstone promptly convinced himself that if he travelled up the Shire he would find another highland plateau that could serve as an alternative fertile, healthy place for his beloved colony.

However, this journey, too, was fraught with problems. Arab and Portuguese slave traders had devastated the area and local tribesmen screamed at the *Ma Robert* from the bank and shot showers of poisoned arrows. The only refuge was down in the horrible hot cabin, which was infested with cockroaches. The cockroaches bred at a terrific rate (once, Livingstone put two females in a jar and 78 little cockroaches hatched) and they ate everything: food, botanical specimens, candles, and the

legs of anyone who tried to sleep. Livingstone intro-
duced a mongoose and several species of spider, but
to no avail. The cabin was so hot and dark and foul
that even the mongoose languished and started to lose
weight.

Livingstone, meanwhile, was moody and uncommu-
nicative. Sometimes he would not speak to his party for
days or even weeks, and just stared blankly down the
river. He knew things were going terribly badly wrong
but somehow couldn't acknowledge this to the others.
He wrote in his diaries that his heart felt 'cold and dead'.
One day, he was standing on deck when a crocodile
dragged a native woman at the water's edge down into
the river and ate her, while her companion screamed
with anguish. Livingstone merely blinked slowly and
went on watching.

Then came Livingstone's next big disappointment: it
turned out that the Shire had its own spate of completely impassable cataracts.

But again Livingstone was not to be deterred. He
went back to Tete to restock and then returned back up
the river, equipped this time to set out on foot when the
steamer could go no further. After several weeks of

walking in circles, the expedition finally reached the source of the Shire, Lake Nyasa.

Livingstone made meticulous maps of the lake. He also noted in his journals how the slave traders had wrecked the area. When the expedition passed through villages, the local people ran into their huts and the children screamed in terror. It was hardly a promising beginning for a colony, but Livingstone's letters home were very optimistic.

But the expedition seemed doomed. By the end of 1859, Livingstone had sacked Richard Thornton for laziness and Thomas Baines for stealing sugar and butter. Meanwhile, George Rae was talking of resigning and the crew were mutinous – at one point Livingstone resorted to drubbing one of his men over the head with a cook's ladle to restore order. And, just to make matters worse, *Ma Robert* was springing leaks everywhere.

Livingstone ordered two new boats from England and while he waited for them to arrive, he turned his attention inland. He spent most of 1860 travelling back into central Africa to take his Makololo porters back home to Linyanti, in central Africa. John Kirk and Charles Livingstone went with him, although both men considered the journey pointless, since few of the Makololo actually wanted to go back, and nearly half of them absconded within days of setting out. During the journey David Livingstone and his brother Charles argued bitterly and came to blows. The rift between the two men never healed.

When Livingstone eventually reached the town of Sesheke, he discovered that Sekeletu was suffering from leprosy. He also heard bad news about the missionary expedition that he had insisted the London Missionary Society send out to the Makololo in Linyanti. At the time, Livingstone had played down the dangers of any expedition, describing the friendliness of the Makololo and stating that malaria, if treated correctly, was 'no worse than a common cold'.

But the two missionary families, who had been assured by the London Missionary Society that Livingstone would be in Linyanti to meet them, had set out on their travels without a doctor and without quinine. They had suffered horribly, with three adults and three children dying of malaria in pitiful circumstances. Only one missionary, Roger Price, and two of the children survived. And the Makololo had not proved so friendly: they had stolen most of the expedition's supplies and dug up Mrs Price's body to use her head for magical purposes.

But, as usual, Livingstone's optimism remained undented. On the return trip to Tete, he decided to try and shoot the first rapids at Kebrabasa. The canoes overturned and John Kirk nearly drowned, losing all his clothes and possessions, including the eight volumes of botanical notes and drawings he had spent the last two years compiling.

Now without their canoes, the party continued on foot. But Charles Livingstone, still angry with his brother, forged on ahead, taking all the food supplies. Livingstone and Kirk only just managed the long journey back to Tete.

**

The following year, things got worse. Thanks to Livingstone's upbeat letters to fundraising bodies back in England, a group of missionaries arrived to start up a settlement in the Shire highlands. They brought with them Livingstone's new steamer *The Pioneer*, which replaced the defunct *Ma Robert*.

Livingstone already knew that the river was shallow and that the lands by the Shire river were blighted by the slave trade. There was also a bitter tribal war underway here between the Ajawa and Mangana people. However, as he had made light of these unfortunate facts in his correspondence and had encouraged the missionaries to come, Livingstone was now obliged to help them. So he took the missionaries up the Shire river in his new steamboat which, just like the old *Ma Robert*, had to be dragged over the sand and mud, sometimes for weeks at a time.

The first thing they did on arrival in the Shire highlands was to release a caravan of slaves, whom they found with their hands tied and their necks bound to long forked pieces of wood called taming sticks. This inevitably drew Livingstone and the missionaries into conflict with the Ajawa tribe who acted as middlemen for the slave traders. The skirmishes worsened and, in July 1861, Livingstone, for the first time in his life, opened fire on Africans. Six Ajawa warriors died in the fighting that day. Livingstone was mortified, but he still let his men burn down an Ajawa village.

Shortly afterwards, Livingstone left the missionaries and went off to chart the coast of Lake Nyasa. Here the Ngoni tribe had been out raiding and Livingstone found he was passing through land littered with skeletons and putrid bodies. Often he could smell a village long before he reached it. And, despite all his medical training, the sickly sweet smell of rotting flesh still made him retch.

Towards the end of 1861, Livingstone headed back to the mouth of the Zambesi to meet the ship carrying Mary Livingstone and the pieces of his second portable steamer, which he aimed to carry up to Lake Nyasa.

Mary Livingstone was meant to have come on the Zambesi expedition from the very start. But on the outbound voyage to Africa she had discovered she was pregnant and so had gone to her parents' settlement in Kuruman where she gave birth to a baby girl, Anna Mary. Then she and the baby had returned to England, where she had spent a couple more miserable years in the Livingstone family cottage in Hamilton. Afterwards, when Livingstone had written asking her to join him, she had left behind all her children, who were by that time either at boarding-school or staying with relatives.

Little Anna Mary, who had never seen her father, was still only three.

And now, four years later, Mary Livingstone had finally arrived to join the expedition. On the deck Livingstone embraced his wife and noticed that she had grown exceedingly stout. It was, he couldn't help noticing, just like putting your arms round a huge tropical tree-trunk – a tropical tree that smelt decidedly of drink.

MARY LIVINGSTONE

Perhaps she had needed brandy to settle her stomach. Livingstone said nothing.

The journey back up the Zambesi river was, as usual, excruciatingly slow and uncomfortable. The *Pioneer*, which was now carrying the huge metal pieces of the new portable steamer, had become so weighed down that the steamer ran aground umpteen times, and the strain on the engine burst the boiler.

Also the portholes were now under the waterline and could not be opened. As a result, David and Mary Livingstone, who were sharing a small, meltingly hot cabin in the stern, had to have a hole drilled into the deck to allow air in.

There were occasional moments of fun and laughter, such as when the men would go hunting and stew up a curry with the day's kill, or the time when the ship's gormless bulldog fell through the skylight and landed with a thunderous splat onto Mary's plate at dinner time. But mostly the mood on board was downcast and nearly everybody fell ill with fever and diarrhoea.

And the Livingstones were not in the best of spirits. David Livingstone – now worried about his portable steamer and the Shire missionaries (two of whom had already died of disease) – was a bad-tempered passenger. Mary Livingstone was a most gloomy one.

Poor Mary Livingstone! For ten years she had had no happiness and no home. Her body, puffed up with too many brandies and marital grudges, had become so fat that she waddled rather than walked. Her hands trembled. Her face was a mass of broken veins – not unlike the river system of central Africa that her husband had been charting for so long.

Mary Livingstone felt sour and angry. When anyone mentioned missionaries or missionary work, she would cast her eyes to the ceiling and give loud, derisive snorts. At night she no longer prayed, and spoke of doubting everything she had once believed in. There was a bleak, hunted look to her eyes that made Livingstone fear that she had lost her faith in God.

Certainly she had given up any hope of a settled happy life, and she told her husband gloomily that she feared they would never have a proper home of their own. Livingstone laughed off the remark claiming she was 'just in one of her moods'. But, sadly, she was proved correct.

Three and a half months after her arrival, when the

Pioneer was moored upriver at the old Portuguese settlement of Shupanga, Mary Livingstone fell ill. She had been out of sorts for some time, but, being used to hardship, she had made light of her condition. Then one morning her skin had turned yellow and she was vomiting every quarter of an hour. Livingstone held the bowl for her and made cheery conversation while she retched and moaned in pain.

There was one deserted stone house at Shupanga and it was here that Livingstone's men arranged packing boxes on the earth floor and placed a mattress on top. Then they carried Mary Livingstone in and laid her down. By now she was delirious and Livingstone was very worried. He gave her huge amounts of quinine, but the fever remained. He and Kirk applied poultices of calomel*, but sweat ran off her till the mattress was sodden. They administered an enema*, which was messy but made no difference. Mary Livingstone's condition worsened.

All that day, through the heat of the midday sun and the long slow afternoon of cooking smells and into the interminable night, Livingstone sat with his wife. He stroked her hand and murmured words of comfort in her ear, but her mind was wandering. She cried out for her children – for Agnes and Oswell and wayward Robert and sickly Tom and especially for the baby of the family, Anna Mary. The hallucinations were horrific. At one point, Livingstone had to hold her down as she screeched and pointed across the room, 'See! See! Agnes is falling down a precipice.'

As the night wore on, Mary Livingstone became stiller. Now she was too weak to raise her head from the pillow, and too weak for any more terrifying visions. Livingstone propped her up in his arms and tried to coax a few slices of melon down her throat – but everything came back up immediately. Soon she could no longer swallow at all.

Dawn broke and Mary Livingstone, with her hair matted and her nightgown sopping wet, slumped into a coma. Now there was no doubt in Livingstone's mind that his wife was dying. No doubt at all. But he agonised about the state of her soul: had her loss of faith been just a momentary aberration or a more permanent state of mind? Was she leaving this world in a state of grace? Or had she, as he feared, turned away from God, to be cast out into eternal darkness and woe?

Livingstone knelt on the ground and commended her spirit to God. But praying was not enough. He knew he had to rouse her. She *must* recover her faith. Even though he realised she would be stone deaf from the quinine, he held her arm tightly and cried out, 'My dearie, my dearie, you are going to leave me. Are you resting on Jesus?' And just for a moment she opened her eyes and looked up.

Mary Livingstone died that evening. In the dank, stuffy room, her husband sat on the side of the bed and wept like a child.

CHAPTER EIGHT

Livingstone never really recovered from his wife's death. He struggled on in Africa for another year until the British government recalled the Zambesi expedition. Then, after miraculously managing to sail his little paddle-steamer across the Indian Ocean to Bombay, he returned to Britain.

Here Livingstone wrote a book about his Zambesi travels. He saw Agnes, Tom and Oswell, who were now all grown beyond recognition, and met for the first time his youngest daughter Anna Mary, a lively little girl of five.

Livingstone's oldest son Robert, who had rebelled against school and his strict religious upbringing, was not at home. He had gone off travelling and ended up, probably against his will, in the American Civil War on the Unionists' side. He died in a prison camp in Carolina a few days before his 19th birthday.

David Livingstone remained in Britain for a year, putting all his affairs in order. There was, however, one painful matter that he neglected. For several years he had been suffering from haemorrhoids*. In Glasgow he consulted a specialist who strongly recommended surgery. But Livingstone refused to have the operation, partly because he feared that the newspapers might make fun of him and partly because it would have meant taking time off to convalesce. Livingstone's decision – and this was a man who had always prided himself on attending to his bowels – was eventually to have terrible consequences.

By 1865 he was in a hurry to return to Africa. For now he had developed a new obsession: he wished to find the source of the Nile. Did the great river start in Lake Victoria? Or did it flow out from Lake Tanganyika? (In fact, Lake Victoria is the source of the Nile.) This age-old mystery preoccupied the Victorian geographers and explorers and, during Livingstone's stay in Britain, it was a hotly debated subject.

So Livingstone set out again for his last great journey.

This was to be a smaller scale and much less ambitious endeavour than the Zambesi expedition. This time there were no European companions, no missionaries, no portable steamers to carry up cataracts, no madcap colonial dreams. Livingstone would travel light, accompanied only by his porters. However, the two journeys did share one thing in common – they were both utter disasters.

The last great expedition began badly. In 1866, Livingstone made his way from the east coast of Africa to Lake Nyasa. This time, instead of trying to reach the lake via the Zambesi, he went overland, walking day after day through burnt, deserted grassland and stunted trees. It was famine land and there was no one – at least no one still alive

For Livingstone was travelling on a slave traders' route, and along the paths he found the corpses of men and women and children who had been too ill or weak to keep up with the slave caravans. Some slaves had been shot, some stabbed, others had simply been tied up and left to starve to death, with their wooden yokes still round their necks.

Livingstone went on, and after nearly six months on

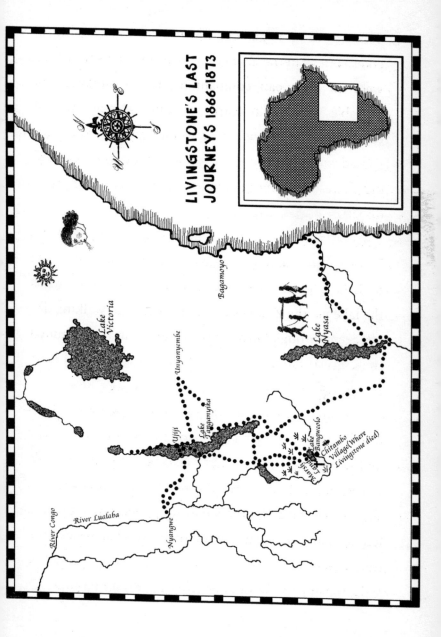

LIVINGSTONE'S LAST JOURNEYS 1866-1873

Bagamoyo

Lake Victoria

Lake Nyasa

Unyanyembe

Ujiji

Lake Tanganyika

Lake Bangweolo

Chitambo Village(Where Livingstone died)

Lake Mweru

River Congo

River Lualaba

Nyangwe

the road, he reached Lake Nyasa. He knew that the source of the Nile was *somewhere* in this region, so for the next five years he was to remain in the African interior, travelling around Lake Nyasa, Lake Tanganyika and other smaller lakes, charting the local waterways and trying to work out how they were all interconnected.

These were the years that turned Livingstone into an old man. For here travelling – or even just surviving – was so difficult. The weather was insufferable: hot, muggy air and weeks and weeks of interminable rain. Then there were the marshes. Some were merely extended puddles, but others were full of black, sticky mud where, with every step, a rush of farty-smelling bubbles burst on to the surface. Sometimes everyone had to walk waist-high carrying the stores on their heads, and every now and then a head would disappear below the surface of the mud when someone trod on an elephant's footprint.

Livingstone's teeth fell out, his pack animals died, the expedition frequently ran short of food, the new supplies coming from Zanzibar were mostly pilfered, many of the porters deserted, and others he fired for laziness or thieving. Having set out with 35 men, Livingstone was soon down to 11. At one particularly low point he had only four faithful retainers.

During these years every sort of misfortune befell him, blow after blow of bad luck in quick, blunt succession. The only interruption came from periods of illness.

January 1867, for example, was a particularly bad month. First, a porter dropped Livingstone's chronometer, and from then on all his longitude readings would be 20 miles too far to the east. (Not long afterwards an earth tremor jogged the mechanism, making it 50 miles out in the opposite direction).

Later in the month, just as everyone began to come down with malaria and dysentery, two men deserted with the medicine chest. Then, when the men were crossing a wide river, Livingstone's fearlessly yappy pet poodle, Chitane, drowned. Finally, Livingstone himself came down with what he thought was rheumatic fever*.

Yet, despite all his trials, Livingstone pressed on. As the years passed, he was gradually gaining a clearer idea of how the lakes and rivers of north east Africa were interconnected. But the process – the endless swamps and rain and the fevers they brought – was gradually killing him.

His sufferings were immense. After rheumatic fever came pneumonia, and with that came hallucinations. He spat blood and coughed day and night. Then, when he seemed to have recovered, the pneumonia returned, accompanied by dysentery and heavy anal bleeding. Afterwards came terrible leg ulcers that opened weeping, crater-like sores in his flesh. For six months he was unable to move and stayed in the little town of Bambarre. The neighbouring tribes were cannibals and ate his boy-assistant James, after he had deserted.

At Bambarre, Livingstone began to go mad. He read the Bible four times from cover to cover, and he became particularly obsessed with the book of Exodus and the legend that Moses had come from this part of Africa. He also pondered interminably about the source of the Nile.

He convinced himself that the answer lay with Herodotus, the ancient Greek historian who wrote of the 'fountains of the Nile' as four springs of water at a point midway between two cone-shaped hills. But where were the four springs? Where were these conical hills?

He quizzed everyone he could, but nobody had heard of them.

Eventually, when the ulcers healed and Livingstone was able to travel again, he made his way to the town of Nyangwe on the banks of the Lualaba river, which he was now completely convinced was the upper reaches of the Nile*.

The local people did not want to give Livingstone passage across the river. So, for three months, he waited, brooding over his Bible and making sketches of fish from the Lualaba so as to compare them with species found down in the lower Nile, in Egypt.

Livingstone also whiled away hours at the market-place. How he loved to watch the women bargaining and laughing with their baskets on their heads. He grew to know the man with the necklace of ten human jawbones round his neck (the man boasted he had eaten all the owners) and the sweet little girl who sold roasted white ants. Here, one sunny morning, he was walking down towards the creek where the Africans moored their canoes, when he heard shots ring out. Three Arab soldiers, who were working for a local slave trader, had opened fire in the marketplace and suddenly the air was filled with screams. Hundreds of people stampeded past Livingstone and dived into the water and the sinking canoes.

The fugitives didn't get far. Immediately another group of Arab soldiers nearby started shooting at the backs of the crowd. Along the water's edge, men and women and children were falling to the ground, stumbling over each other. Those that made it into the water mostly drowned or were picked off by the gunmen.

Although nobody was fighting back, the Arab soldiers continued firing round after round, and soon the ground was strewn with bodies. Some had escaped, and there were swimmers out in the middle of the river, but soon these heads bobbing in the water started disappearing below the surface. On and on and on went the killing.

Livingstone, who had taken cover at the side of a hut, stared fixedly ahead. He had witnessed horrifying events before – he had seen one of his own children die and at medical school in Glasgow he had watched plenty of operations performed without anaesthetic – but he had never seen anything quite on this scale. Hundreds of people were screaming all at once, hundreds were dying.

The gunshots cracked on through the hot, dusty air.

'This is a massacre. This is a massacre,' Livingstone said to himself over and over again. He tried to count the victims – 400 souls? 500? Maybe it was more. He couldn't be sure; his mind felt fuzzy. The dying seemed to have sucked up all the air around him. Livingstone crouched on the ground, open-mouthed, gasping like a fish.

***

Disgusted with the Arab slave traders, Livingstone left Nyangwe after a few days and started on the long, gruelling journey back to Ujiji on the banks of Lake Tanganyika. Here he hoped to pick up the new supplies that he had ordered from Zanzibar.

Three months later, an exhausted Livingstone finally arrived in Ujiji, only to find that, yet again, his supplies had been stolen. Now he had nothing – no medicines, no money, no beads, no brass wire, just a few rolls of calico that he had wisely left with a friend. He was ill and destitute and knew he wouldn't survive long without help.

But, as had happened so often in Livingstone's life,

help arrived just in time. For it was now, only a few days after his arrival in Ujiji, that the ambitious young journalist Henry Morton Stanley appeared in his crisp white suit, doffed his pith helmet and uttered his greeting, 'Dr Livingstone, I presume?'

Stanley brought Livingstone food, medicine, brandy, packages of letters and back issues of *Punch* magazine. Livingstone in return would bring Stanley lasting fame and riches (he later wrote a bestseller entitled *How I Found Livingstone*). So it was only natural that the two men should have become instant friends.

Stanley, instead of returning immediately to the coast to write up his scoop, stayed on with Livingstone for five months. They explored the northern shores of Lake Tanganyika together. Then, before Stanley left, he tried to convince Livingstone to return to Europe with him to regain his strength and have a set of false teeth fitted. But the explorer wouldn't listen. He was still determined to find Herodotus's fountains of the Nile.

And eventually, after a long wait for Stanley to send more supplies and more men, Livingstone set off again on his wanderings. Now he was heading south along the eastern shore of Lake Tanganyika, climbing up and down hills and valleys where the ground was so hot that the porters burned their bare feet.

In October, Livingstone contracted fever and dysentery. Then, in November, came the great rains and a new onslaught of anal bleeding. By December, Livingstone was often too weak to walk and his men were carrying him on their shoulders over the endless swamps of Lake Bangweolo. January 1873 meant more endless swamps. By now, Livingstone was completely lost and had stopped believing the bearings on his chronometer. For it seemed that the rains and the flooding rivers had washed away any landmarks and all that could be seen was water, reeds and ant-hills.

In February there was more of the same, and Livingstone was getting weaker every day. The internal bleeding never seemed to stop and every few hours he would have to change the blood-soaked padding in his breeches. He was always surprised by the flood of red – it felt as if there were a tiny man with a hydraulic pump in his lower intestines drawing out his blood by the bucketful.

The days dragged on: all grey skies and rain and never quite enough to eat. In fact it was just like his childhood in Blantyre – except this was worse in that he had bowel problems and his bedding was always wet.

The monotony seemed unending, but then one February night something most unpleasant interrupted the tedium. That night Livingstone was in his grass hut. He had already gone through his usual evening rituals: he had plucked the leeches off his legs, prayed, written up his diary, changed the padding in his drawers and lain down on his trestle bed. This last act was difficult – he had to keep all his weight off the excruciatingly painful area in his lower back where the tiny man with the hydraulic pump seemed to live. But finally Livingstone had got himself comfortable and was just drifting to sleep when he heard the first shouts and screams of horror. A minute later he heard someone crashing through the reeds, and the splash as a body hit the water. More crashes and shouts followed. His men were clearly running in all directions.

Livingstone sat up on his trestle, lit a candle and looked over at the door. Creeping swiftly towards him was a thick, red snake. The snake made a strange crackling noise, like a ball of paper being crunched up. A snake that *crackled*? Surely not. Livingstone blinked hard and look again. No. It was not a snake. These were red driver ants. Thousands and thousands of ants coming across the earth floor towards his bed.

Remembering the famous missionary, Dr Van der Kemp, who claimed that 'no animal will attack man if unprovoked', Livingstone sat very still and watched, completely fascinated, as the advancing army moved up the leg of the trestle bed. He estimated their speed (about three miles an hour) and noted how, in their rush, the ants scurried on top of each other, just as the poor victims had done during the massacre at Nyangwe.

When the ants reached his feet, Livingstone realised his mistake. Dr Van der Kemp clearly hadn't known about driver ants. For the vanguard of the army suddenly attacked the soft, vulnerable skin between Livingstone's toes. Then larger ants advanced up his feet nipping furiously until the blood spurted out. Livingstone was impressed: so small and yet what a bite to them!

How did they do it? The ants were up to Livingstone's knees now so it was easier for him to bend over and watch their technique. Firstly, the ant would jab the skin with two very sharp curved mandibles, then its six little legs would swivel round and, working like a lever, apply more pressure. So clever! So effective! So painful!

Livingstone knew it was time to move. He staggered out of the hut, with the ants now swarming over his entire body, covering his mouth and eyes, exploring his scalp and making their way inside his ears. He felt as if his body was on fire – he was being bitten everywhere all at once. But he could not cry out with pain, for he knew that if he did so, the ants would be crawling down his gullet in a trice.

Livingstone tried to brush the creatures off but, as soon as he did so, fresh ants immediately took their place. His faithful servants Susi and Chuma ran up and started to help pull the ants off. They called to others to help and soon there was a crowd around Livingstone, some pulling the insects off him, others running up with bundles of lighted straw which they dropped on the hoards of insects on the ground.

It took two hours before the ants retreated and Livingstone, bitten raw all over, was helped into an ant-free hut and left to rest. He had barely closed his eyes, when he heard a horribly familiar crackling sound. Something was coming through the door This time Livingstone didn't stop to watch.

***

Livingstone and his men moved on. March passed and April came but still they were plodding their way over the same great flat expanse of water, scattered with ant-hills and occasional patches of higher ground. It was a most desolate landscape, with only the whispering of wind in the rushes and the eerie screech of the fish eagle. These birds haunted Livingstone – they sounded as if they were crying out to someone in another world.

And Livingstone knew the end was near. His intestines were in agony and he couldn't bear even the faintest pressure on his lower back. But he was still determined to find the four fountains of the Nile and he wrote in his diary: 'Nothing earthly will make me give up my work in despair. I encourage myself in the Lord my God and go forwards.'

By late April, Livingstone was too weak and ill to travel – so his men made him a stretcher or 'kitanda', covered it with grass and a blanket, and carried him on through the marshes. Then, one morning, Livingstone could no longer get from his bed to the door of his grass hut, so Susi and Chuma pulled down the wall of the hut and brought the kitanda to their master's bedside. That day, with Livingstone groaning and delirious with pain, the men marched on, until at last they reached the edge of the Bangweolo marshes. They stopped a few miles beyond at Chief Chitambo's village.

Here in the drizzle, Susi and Chuma made a hut of reeds and grass and laid Livingstone down to rest. Chief Chitambo came early the next morning to pay his respects, but Livingstone was too weak to talk and just lay drifting in and out of consciousness. At one point he asked Susi to bring him his watch, and he showed his manservant how to hold the watch while he slowly wound it up. But even the effort of winding a watch exhausted Livingstone and he flopped back down onto his bed and slept.

That night – 30th April 1873 – the men built a fire in front of Livingstone's hut. Late in the evening he called for Susi and asked him to bring boiling water and his medicine box. Susi lit a candle – for Livingstone's sight was failing – and with slow, shaking hands the dying man picked out a bottle of calomel*.

Then, when Susi had poured out some water, Livingstone said in a feeble voice. 'All right, you can go out now.' These were to be his last words.

Some time after midnight the errand boy Majwara dropped off to sleep by the fire. At four o'clock in the morning the boy woke with a jolt of cold premonition. It was the darkest part of the night and the fire at his feet was now just dull embers, but a faint light came from his master's hut where a candle was still burning.

Majwara crept forward to the door of the hut and looked in. Livingstone was kneeling in prayer by his bed-side, with his head buried in his hands and his body propped forwards onto a pillow.

Majwara was frightened. Before he had gone to sleep, he had noticed that his master was down on his knees praying. Since then a good part of the night had passed. Majwara looked again.

He couldn't see his master's face – it was hidden in his hands. But the praying man in the candlelight, did have a certain stillness about him. And it was the still-ness of a statue, not of a man contemplating his God. There was no movement of air in the hut. Nobody was breathing.

Majwara ran to wake Chuma and Susi. The great explorer David Livingstone was dead.

POSTCRIPT

Livingstone once wrote in his diary that he wanted his grave 'to lie in the still, still forest and no hand ever to disturb [his] bones'.

But this was not to be. When Livingstone died, Susi and Chuma decided that he must be returned to his homeland and, in order to do so, they set about preserving his body.

After a funeral in Chitambo, Livingstone's abdomen was cut open and his innards removed. The men noted a blood clot the size of a man's hand resting in Livingstone's lower intestines – and this must have accounted for the agonising pain he had suffered in the last weeks of life. Livingstone's heart and other organs were put in a tin box, previously used for storing flour. These remains were buried with a short ceremony.

Livingstone had been little more than skin and bones when he died and the dry season had started, so preserving the rest of the body was quite easy. The men placed salt in the abdominal cavity, poured some brandy in the mouth and rubbed the rest into his scalp. Then they left the body out to dry for two weeks, turning it every day. Afterwards, they bent the legs back to make a more compact package, wrapped the corpse first in calico, and then in a cylindrical piece of bark. They covered the bark in sailcloth, coated the sailcloth with tar and fixed the pack to a pole so that it could be carried on the shoulders of two men.

It took Livingstone's party nine months to bring his body back across Africa, and ten of his men died during the journey. In Zanzibar, the corpse was transferred to a zinc-lined coffin, and then shipped to England. When Livingstone's coffin was opened at the Royal Geographical Society in London, a doctor was able to identify the mummified corpse as Livingstone's because of the huge lump in the bone where his left arm had been shattered by the lion in Mabotsa 30 years earlier.

On 18th April 1874, almost a year after his death, a day of national mourning was announced in Britain, and Livingstone was finally put to rest in Westminster Abbey. Today his bones lie in the centre of the main aisle of the abbey in front of the tomb of the Unknown Soldier.

But his heart is still in Africa.

APPENDIX

p.8. Obituaries – short biographies of public figures who have recently died.

p.8. Pagaree – a removable piece of cloth that hangs down from a helmet and protects the back of the neck from the sun.

p.9. Caravan – a group of people travelling together for safety reasons.

p.11. Earth closet – an old-fashioned outside lavatory.

p.12. Tract – a religious document.

p.15. Staines – Scottish dialect pronunciation of 'stones'.

p.18. Uvula – the small lobe of flesh at the back of the mouth.

p.20. Savannah – a large flat stretch of land with short vegetation and very few trees (or none at all) in tropical and sub-tropical Africa.

p.30. Suppurated – oozed with pus.

p.30. Setswana – a language still spoken by more than three million people in Botswana, South Africa, Namibia and Zimbabwe.

p.36. Meal – grain or pulses ground to powder.

p.43. Polygamy – having more than one wife at the same time.

p.44. Quinine – a colourless, odourless, bitter liquid once widely used to treat malaria.

p.50. Springboks – South African antelopes which leap when frightened.

p.50. Gnus – large antelopes which look a bit like horses and buffalos. Also called 'wildebeest'.

p.58. Sextant – an instrument used for navigation, part of it having an arc of 60°.

p.58. Chronometer – an instrument for accurately measuring time.

p.61. Broiled – cooked over hot coals.

p.65. Manioc – a sort of porridge meal, obtained from the root of the cassava plant.

p.66. Baize – a coarse woollen cloth.

p.68. Calabash – the shell of the fruit of the calabash tree.

p.81. Cataract – a huge waterfall.

p.103. Calomel – the name of a liquid which gives you diarrhoea in order to clean out your intestines.

p.103. Enema – fluid or medicine inserted into the anus.

p.107. Haemorrhoids – swollen veins in the rectum, also known as piles, which can bleed and be painful.

p.111. Rheumatic fever – a serious bacterial disease that weakens the heart.

p.113. Upper reaches of the Nile – Livingstone was wrong. The Lualaba river is one of the tributaries of the River Congo.